The
WORST-CASE SCENARIO
Survival Handbook:
WEDDINGS

The
WORST-CASE SCENARIO
Survival Handbook:
WEDDINGS

By Joshua Piven, David Borgenicht, and Sarah Jordan
Illustrations by Brenda Brown

CHRONICLE BOOKS

SAN FRANCISCO

Library of Congress Cataloging-in-Publication Data available.

ISBN: 0-8118-4537-0

Manufactured in the United States of America

Typeset in Adobe Caslon, Bundesbahn Pi, and Zapf Dingbats

Designed by Frances J. Soo Ping Chow
Illustrations by Brenda Brown

A **QUIRK** Book
www.quirkpackaging.com
Visit www.worstcasescenarios.com

Distributed in Canada by Raincoast Books
9050 Shaughnessy Street
Vancouver, British Columbia V6P 6E5

10 9 8 7 6 5 4 3 2 1

Chronicle Books LLC
85 Second Street
San Francisco, California 94105
www.chroniclebooks.com

WARNING

When a life is imperiled or a dire situation is at hand, safe alternatives may not exist. To deal with the wedding worst-case scenarios presented in this book, we highly recommend—insist, actually—that the best course of action is to consult a professionally trained expert. But because highly trained professionals may not always be available when the safety or sanity of individuals is at risk, we have asked experts on various subjects to describe the techniques they might employ in these emergency situations. THE PUBLISHER, AUTHORS, AND EXPERTS DISCLAIM ANY LIABILITY from any injury that may result from the use, proper or improper, of the information contained in this book. We do not guarantee that the information contained herein is complete, safe, or accurate, nor should it be considered a substitute for your good judgment, your common sense, or the advice of your mother and/or wedding planner. And finally, nothing in this book should be construed or interpreted to infringe on the rights of other persons or to violate criminal statutes; we urge you to obey all laws and respect all rights, including property rights, of others, even your new in-laws.

—The Authors

CONTENTS

"For better or for worse . . ."

INTRODUCTION

Your wedding day is going to be the best, most wonderful day of your life, if you believe what you've been told by your family, friends, romantic novels, soap operas, movie musicals, and countless magazines that sell fashion and lifestyle.

And it is entirely possible that it's true—there is indeed something magical and transforming about standing in front of the people you love and know best and declaring your endless devotion and commitment to your soul mate.

On the other hand, why should everything go right? Just because you want it to? There's more than a passing chance that the wedding reception is costing way more than you budgeted. That the band won't show up. Your wedding gown or tuxedo will be too tight, or something will spill on it. Your in-laws will hate you. A friend of the groom's will offer a truly offensive toast. A fight will break out between the guests. Or simply that the stress of the event will be too much for you to handle.

For some reason, and it's been true since the first exchange of vows in front of an audience, people become quintessentially themselves at weddings. Whatever tendencies and quirks they regularly have become wildly exaggerated, even more so if they are in the wedding party. Think of the shortcomings and annoying habits of everyone on your guest list—including yourself and your spouse—and expect to see those traits in spades. Is someone rude? Is someone else a hypochondriac? Have a relative who is self-centered? Invite anyone who is mean spirited? Know anyone who likes to drink too much?

Now you're beginning—but just beginning—to grasp why we felt it necessary to prepare you for the full range of worst-case wedding scenarios.

By comparison with what comes next, deciding to get married is the easiest step: all you have to do is say yes. One person asks one question, the other person gives a one-word answer: done. But then, almost immediately, other questions pour out—beginning with when and where—and you and your betrothed are caught up in a vortex of decisions, uncertainty, complications, and the realization that lots of things could go wrong.

Whether your wedding is a formal affair, inventive and exotic, or laid-back and casual, you can't escape one fundamental fact: Every bride and groom experience significant tension during the planning phase of the wedding. It's simple. If you didn't care about these people, about whether they'd attend and what kind of time they'd have, you wouldn't be having a wedding reception in the first place. And so okay, you've decided to have a reception, but who pays for it, and whom do you invite? That leads to endless discussions about picking the menu, the band, the bridesmaid dresses, and the flowers—and remember that stress causes insomnia, pimples, rashes, strains on relationships, and an increased likelihood of accidents.

Weddings seem to be designed for accidents anyway. Who decided that veils, trains, and high heels go together, especially when they are to be worn by someone who is excited, moving around a lot, and possibly drinking champagne?

If you haven't already paid the caterer, you may still be able to elope: Grab a few things, run out the door, and get hitched in front of a court officer and witnesses you've never met before and will never see again. You would be reducing some of the risks covered by this book, but not all of them. You still are not safe. You cannot stop reading.

As with our previous *Worst-Case Scenario Survival Handbooks,* we've consulted dozens of highly trained professionals in the hope that we can preempt a nuptial nightmare. We spoke with florists, public speaking consultants, chefs, emergency medical physicians, wedding planners, dentists, nutritionists, sexologists, and dozens of other highly trained professionals who have provided step-by-step answers to the most likely nightmare scenarios within.

This handbook takes you chronologically through the wedding process, from planning to the honeymoon, from surviving a bachelor or bachelorette party to treating wedding day–related injuries, from finding a groom who has gone missing to making emergency rings. We've even included an appendix with a handy Gift Evaluator/Thank-You Note Generator.

So forget about something borrowed, something blue. When you walk down the aisle, carry this book. Here's to the happy bride and groom.

—The Authors

CHAPTER 1

PRENUPTIAL
SURVIVAL SKILLS

HOW TO RAISE MONEY FOR THE WEDDING

★ **Ask family members to pay for specific expenses.**
Have numbers ready to justify costs. If you sense resistance, threaten to elope or to have the reception at a seedy nightclub. For grandparents, offer upgrades at the reception in exchange for funding, such as seating at a table far from the band, their food served first, or wider, cushioned seats.

★ **Register for wedding ceremony and reception components.**
Instead of a bridal registry for china, crystal, and silver, register for floral arrangements, the band, limousine service, liquor for the reception, and each course of the meal.

★ **Hold a raffle.**
Offer the guests a chance to buy tickets to win the wedding dress, a ride in the limo, or a chance to join the honeymoon.

★ **Wash guests' cars.**
Hire a student at a low hourly rate to sell expensive car washes to the guests as they attend the ceremony and reception.

Procure sponsors to help defray costs.

★ **Sell your belongings on Internet auction sites.**
Check to see which items you've registered for have been bought, or estimate which items you are sure to receive, and sell them online. The buyer will send payment, and, after the wedding, you send the sold item.

★ **Procure sponsors.**
Strike a deal with a local company. Agree to place its logo on the invitation, wedding dress, tuxedo, or cake. Have the band leader announce each song with, "This song has been brought to you by the good people at *[name of company]*." Hang company banners around the altar and behind the bandstand. Allow the company to set up a kiosk at the ceremony and reception site to dispense information, key chains, and other swag.

★ **Sell incentive packages to investors.**
Offer a percentage of wedding gifts, naming rights to kids, occasional dinners at your home, an invitation to the wedding (with preferred seating), the first dance with the bride/groom, and, for enough money, the opportunity to give away the bride.

HOW TO MAKE YOUR BETROTHED'S PARENTS LIKE YOU

⭐ **Be direct.**
Have a conversation about your feelings. Start with, "I've noticed a change in our relationship, and I was wondering if I have done something to offend." Talk about the issue from your point of view. Use phrases such as "I feel this" as opposed to "you did this" so they will not feel attacked. Listen carefully and remain open to criticism.

⭐ **Be nice.**
Remain pleasant and respectful, and you will eventually wear them down. Be patient, as this might take some time.

⭐ **Arrange for testimonials.**
Ask friends, relatives, and neighbors to vouch for your value as a human being when your future in-laws come to visit. Leave information packets on their pillows that include letters of recommendation from coaches, employers, teachers, and religious and community leaders. Include a pie chart that expresses the amount of time you devote each day to your future spouse.

★ Volunteer your services.
Help with household tasks such as changing the kitty litter, caulking the tub, or walking the dog at the crack of dawn. Take them to the airport at rush hour, teach your betrothed's younger siblings how to drive, install their new computer system, re-point the brick exterior of their home, prepare their tax returns, refinish the floors throughout their house, and detail their car.

★ Find a common bond.
If your in-laws dislike you because they do not know you, invite them out together or separately on outings they enjoy. If your mother-in-law likes tea, ask her to tea. If she prefers the theater, take her to a play. Take your father-in-law golfing, or if he's a man of few words, to the movies or a nightclub. Pick up the tab.

★ Plant a diary where your in-laws will be sure to find it.
Fill the diary with virtuous thoughts and aspirations. Declare your love for your betrothed repeatedly. Add entries about how much you like your future in-laws and how much you hope they'll like you, too.

★ Pretend you are friends with celebrities.
Find out who their heroes are (politicians, authors, activists, sports figures, movie stars, etc.) and autograph and frame a glossy photo of a celebrity to yourself. Mention to your future in-laws you might be able to pull a few strings if they'd like to meet the famous person.

★ Pay for the wedding.
If you or your family are already paying for the wedding, offer to pay off their mortgage or car payments.

★ Let them move in.
Give them the big bathroom.

★ Promise to provide them with a grandchild within a negotiated period of time.

HOW TO DEAL WITH AN OVERBEARING MOTHER-IN-LAW

★ Say yes, mean no.
Agree with everything your future mother-in-law says when you are together, but do what you wish when she is gone. Just nod at her sweetly and pat her on the shoulder when she says or does something inappropriate. If she later asks about decisions, say you and your future spouse discussed it further and you hope she understands.

★ Hire/designate a fake professional.
Get a friend or an actor to impersonate a wedding planner, and have your mother-in-law share her ideas with him. When her ideas aren't executed, blame the fake planner.

★ Blame your bladder.
Leave the room when her difficult nature flares. Apologize, appear mildly embarrassed, and say you need to use the bathroom. Drink plenty of water and other fluids when in her presence so your exits appear justified.

★ Send her on useless missions.
Instruct her to meet with vendors you have no intention of using. Match her up with notoriously difficult

florists, bandleaders, caterers, and other wedding suppliers.

Be Aware

Mothers-in-law have a tendency to pull something at the last minute, just when you thought you had safely made it to the day of the wedding. Be on guard for her claims of illness—dizziness, nausea, diarrhea—that shift the focus of attention to her. Be especially prepared for the most common stunt, inappropriate wedding attire that:

- shows too much cleavage
- is more appropriate for a funeral
- steals the show (bright red)
- flaunts her own wedding dress (especially if she is recently divorced)

To avoid the surprise dress, ask well before the wedding to see what she will be wearing.

HOW TO TRIM THE GUEST LIST

1 Determine your budget.
Decide the maximum amount of guests you can afford to invite or who will fit at the wedding site.

2 Make lists.
The bride, groom, and respective parents each should make a list of people to invite.

3 Strike as many people as you can from your own list.

4 Remove unnecessary names from someone else's list. Take turns striking one name at a time from the list of the person sitting to your right. If that person objects to the removal of the potential invitee, invoke the "two strikes" rule and find an ally to vote against the would-be guest. Remove contested names that have two votes against them. (There are variations on the rule that grant people paying for the entire wedding greater voting power: Their vote for removal counts as three votes, and the names on their list are untouchable.)

5 Compile a master list.
Combine the remaining names and organize them by category: wedding party, work contacts, relations, friends, parents' friends, college friends, others. Each person at the table should rank each person within a

category by importance, as determined by the answers to the following questions:

- How often have we seen this person in the last year?
- Did he really seem glad to see us?
- If I invite this person, will I be obligated to invite his spouse or friends?
- How much power does this person hold over me?
- How rich is he and will he use his wealth for good gifts?
- Will he seem impressive to my friends?
- Is he good looking? Will he improve my wedding photos or video?
- Can I handle the fallout if I do not invite him?

6 Agree in advance what the cut-off level will be. Remove entire categories. Decide no kids, no work-related people, no relations beyond first cousins, no dates for singles, no redheads.

7 Remove people below a certain rank.

8 Create barriers to attendance. Make it impossible for large numbers of people to attend.

- Hold the wedding in the middle of the week.
- Hold the wedding at a distant location (Antarctica, tiny Pacific island).
- Require formal attire or elaborate, expensive costumes.
- Hold the wedding at an inconvenient time (2 A.M.).

9 | Recalculate the list.
Estimate how many people each barrier will knock out. If your list is still too large for your budget, continue to step 10.

10 | Alternate knocking people off the list.
Only the bride and groom (advice from parents is acceptable) take turns removing individual names from the master list until they reach the desired number of guests. If this process becomes too heated, proceed to the next step.

11 | Play Rock, Paper, Scissors.
The winner of each round can eliminate a name or add someone back onto the list.

Be Aware

- Send out the invitations six to eight weeks before the event. As you get negative responses, send out your "B list" invitations to people who didn't make the cut. Stop sending invitations out a month before the wedding date; last-minute invitees will realize their status and be insulted.

- Manage expectations among potential guests.
Let it be known that you plan on a small wedding so that no one is really expecting to be invited. If an invitation arrives, the invitee will be deeply flattered, but those who are not invited will not be hurt—at least that's the theory.

Consider all important factors when trimming your list.

- You are expected to include spouses, fiancés, or long-term live-in companions of your guests. If a guest is only casually dating, you are not obligated to extend an invitation to his date.
- If you forget to invite someone, the next time you see them act annoyed with them for not sending back the RSVP card.

HOW TO SURVIVE THE BACHELOR PARTY

HOW TO PICK A LOCK (WHEN HANDCUFFED TO A BOWLING BALL)

A classic bachelor party prank uses a bowling ball and handcuffs to translate literally the expression "the old ball and chain."

1 Locate a pick.
A handcuff lock can be picked relatively easily with a piece of metal bent into the shape of a key. Whatever you use, the material must be resilient because the springs on a handcuff lock are strong. Use any of the following items:
- Mini screwdriver
- Large paper clip
- Any tough wire (e.g., chicken or piano)
- Small fork
- Hairpin

2 Bend a few millimeters of one end of your pick 90 degrees.

3 Insert the pick into the lock.
Fit the bend into the lock at the point where the nipple of the key fits. You will feel the bend move into place.

4 Turn the pick to open the lock.

Turn the pick left and then right. If the pick won't move, put the latch end of the handcuff vertically on a hard surface and press down. This may relieve a bit of pressure off the lock and make it easier to turn. Be careful, though: Pushing too hard may lock the cuff another tooth and restrict your hand movement.

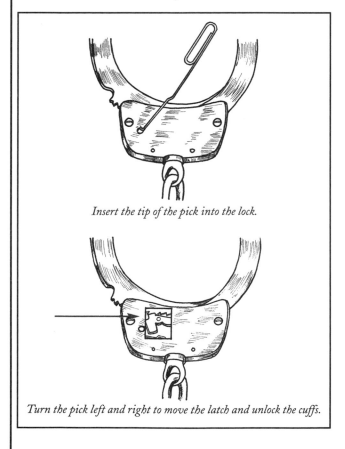

Insert the tip of the pick into the lock.

Turn the pick left and right to move the latch and unlock the cuffs.

How to Smoke a Cigar

1 Clip the head.
The head, or smoking end, of the cigar is covered by a small area of leaf called the cap. Using a sharp cigar cutter, quickly make a guillotine cut, removing a small section ($1/4$ inch or less) of the cap. Do not cut below the end of the cap, or the wrapper may come apart. If no cigar cutter is available, punch a hole in the cap using the tip of a pen or pencil.

2 Hold the cigar in your nondominant hand.

3 Ignite a torch lighter or a long wooden match.
Do not put the cigar to your lips.

4 Toast the end.
Carefully move the flame to the foot (end) while rotating the cigar slowly. This will ensure an even burn. The foot should ignite thoroughly and evenly.

5 When the foot is lit, bring the cigar to your lips.

6 Draw smoke into your mouth.
Suck the smoke through the cigar slowly and evenly while still holding the flame an inch or two from the foot.

7 Puff gently until the foot is completely lit.
Do not inhale the smoke into your lungs.

8 | Exhale.
Savor the flavor of the cigar in your mouth for a few seconds before expelling the smoke.

9 | Repeat steps 7 and 8.
Take one or two draws from the cigar per minute, but do not rush. Rotate the cigar slowly in your fingers or allow it to sit in an ashtray between draws. Keep the foot elevated to maintain an even burn. Avoid squeezing the cigar.

10 | Flick the ash.
Allow half an inch to an inch of ash to accumulate on the foot. Tap the cigar gently with a finger to make the ash fall. Many cigar smokers will try to get the ash as long as possible before flicking it. However, you should flick the ash if you feel it is about to fall and burn a hole in clothing or furniture.

11 | Extinguish the cigar.
Many smokers will discard a cigar when half to three-quarters has been smoked. A quality cigar may be smoked as long as its flavor is still pleasing and the smoke is cool enough to be comfortable in your mouth.

Be Aware

- A *natural*—a cigar with a light brown wrapper— is mild and is more appropriate for beginners. (A *maduro*, or a cigar with a dark brown wrapper, will be rich and full flavored, but may be too harsh for a novice smoker.)

- The wrapper should not be dry, flaking, or crack when handled.
- Gently squeeze the cigar. It should be firm and give lightly to the touch, then regain its shape. A moist cigar has been overhumidified and will not draw well.
- While it may be socially frowned upon, a cigar may be extinguished and relit. Scoop or blow all carbon from the foot of the cigar before relighting, or cut the cigar just above the burned section.

HOW TO SURVIVE THE BRIDAL SHOWER

How to Make a Toilet Paper Dress

Most bridal showers include group games. A game that the bride and her guests are often asked to play involves breaking into groups and dressing several models in toilet paper to see who can create the best bridal gown.

1 Construct the bodice.
- Unwrap a roll of toilet paper around the model's midsection, beginning at her waist and wrapping around her torso, in overlapping layers, until she is wrapped to just underneath her underarms.
- Without detaching the paper, make a small sleeve by wrapping from underneath one of her arms to over and around the opposite shoulder. Repeat over the other shoulder to give the dress a slightly off-the-shoulder neckline.

2 Make the skirt.
- Tape the free end of a fresh roll to the waist on the dress's bodice, unrolling a strip long enough to reach the floor (or your desired length—a short dress can also be nice, especially if your model is wearing a mini skirt or shorts).
- Tape the next piece to the waist of the dress, overlapping to about the middle of the first strip. Unroll to meet the length of the first strip.

- Repeat in this way until you've taped strips the whole way around the model's waist.
- A staggered effect, with strips of different lengths, can earn extra points for creativity.

3 Make a belt.
Unroll several layers of toilet paper directly around the model's waist, to cover the area where the skirt is taped to the bodice of the dress.

4 Make the veil.
- Unwrap about four feet of toilet paper.
- Fold it in half, so that it's two feet long, and then in half again.
- Now fold it lengthwise several times, until you have a fairly sturdy, thick strip to use as a head-band. Tape the sides of the headband to secure it.
- Tape several three- to five-foot-long strips of toilet paper to the headband. The length of the strips can be adjusted to suit your preference.
- Use bobby pins to secure the veil to the model's head.

How to Make a Bow Bouquet

As the bride unwraps her presents, a member of the wedding party is responsible for making a bow bouquet for the bride to carry at her wedding rehearsal. You will need a paper plate; a pencil, pen, or other long skinny object; tape; and bows and ribbons from gifts.

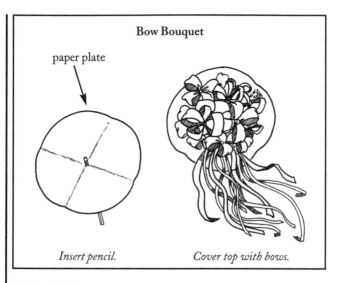

Bow Bouquet

paper plate

Insert pencil.　　　*Cover top with bows.*

1　Make the base.

Fold a paper plate in quarters, then unfold. (The folds in the plate will provide the bow bouquet with volume.) Insert the pencil, pen, or other long skinny object into the center of the plate, push it through so that only about an inch shows through the top, and tape it in place at the top and bottom.

2　Build the bouquet.

As the bride unwraps her gifts, take each bow and ribbon and tape it on top of the plate. Place smaller bows in the center, and larger bows on the outside. Wrap long, curling ribbons around the pencil, allowing them to hang down from under the plate. If the bride has a lot of presents, layer the bows as necessary. Be sure to use all of the bows and ribbons.

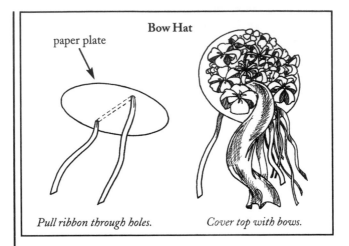

Bow Hat

paper plate

Pull ribbon through holes.   *Cover top with bows.*

Alternate Method:

In some cases, the bows and ribbons from the bride's gifts are used to make a bow hat rather than a bouquet. To make a bow hat:

- Poke a hole about half an inch from the edge of a paper plate. Repeat on the opposite side.
- Thread a thick, wide ribbon through one of the holes, tying a knot at the end on top of the plate to keep it from slipping out. Repeat on the opposite side, leaving the bottom ends loose to tie the hat to the bride's head.
- Tape bows and ribbons to the top of the paper plate so that the largest bows are around the outside edge, the smallest in the center. Attach all long ribbons to hang down from the back of the hat.
- Tie the hat to the bride's head with the two wide ribbons at the sides. Laugh. Cry.

HOW TO KEEP THE BRIDE AND GROOM FROM SEEING EACH OTHER BEFORE THE WEDDING

If the bride and groom are already living together, special measures are required to avoid seeing each other before the ceremony on the day of the wedding.

⭐ **Stay out all night partying.**
Since the wedding day—and the start of the prohibition on seeing each other—begins at midnight, one or both should stay out partying all night (at different clubs). The next day, the bride and groom should go right to where they will be married.

⭐ **Stay with the best man and maid of honor.**
Spend the night sleeping at the home of the main support players in the wedding, as long as they don't live together.

⭐ **Establish a schedule.**
Agree on a timetable that prevents the bride and groom from being in the same room at the same time. For example, the groom will use the bathroom at 10:30 A.M. and the bride at 11:00 A.M.

Wear sleep masks.

Hang a bundling blanket to avoid visual contact.

★ Stay in different rooms in a hotel.

★ Stay home and use escorts.
You should each have a friend stay overnight to guide you and your soon-to-be spouse through the house, checking that the coast is clear before you venture into shared spaces.

★ Maintain mobile phone contact.
Stay home and in constant communication so your paths do not cross.

★ Wear bells.
The noise from the bells will warn the other person of your presence.

★ Wear blindfolds.

★ Hang a divider between you in bed.
Create a bundling blanket or board by hanging a blanket from a line strung over the bed. Alternatively, attach the blanket to the ceiling, as long as it reaches the bed and provides visual protection.

CHAPTER 2

WEDDING DAY EMERGENCIES

HOW TO CONCEAL WEDDING DAY BLEMISHES

DARK CIRCLES UNDER EYES

1 Make two cold compresses.
Place a handful of ice in a plastic bag. Wrap the bag in a cloth napkin or other fabric. Repeat for the other eye.

2 Sit up straight.
Keep your head elevated above your heart—do not lie down before applying the compresses.

3 Apply compresses.
Hold the compresses on the eyes for 10 minutes.

4 Check under the eyes.
If the bags remain, continue to step 5.

5 Steep two tea bags in warm (not boiling) water for 2 minutes.
Black tea is most effective, but any variety of non-herbal tea will suffice. Tannic acid, which reduces swelling, is not present in herbal teas.

6 Place the tea bags in ice water to cool.

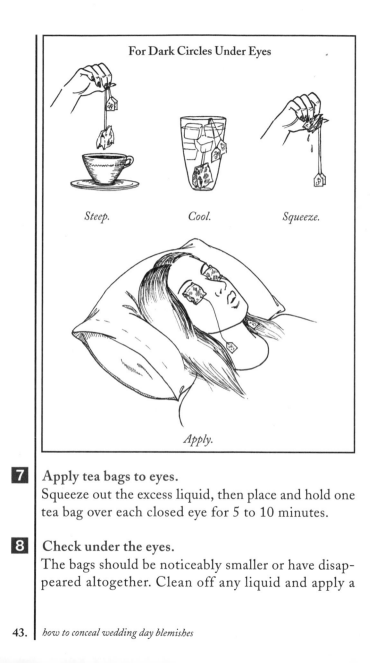

For Dark Circles Under Eyes

Steep.   *Cool.*   *Squeeze.*

Apply.

7 Apply tea bags to eyes.
Squeeze out the excess liquid, then place and hold one tea bag over each closed eye for 5 to 10 minutes.

8 Check under the eyes.
The bags should be noticeably smaller or have disappeared altogether. Clean off any liquid and apply a

layer of under-eye concealer one shade lighter than your foundation if the lids are recessed, and one shade darker than your foundation if they are puffy.

Be Aware

Hemorrhoid ointment may be used to reduce swelling and tighten skin under the eyes. Apply carefully to the affected area and allow to remain for 5 to 10 minutes. Wash your face thoroughly, keeping your eyes closed. Note that hemorrhoid ointment may contain fish oils, which leave a displeasing odor.

PIMPLE

1 Apply a warm compress.
Soak a hand towel, handkerchief, or cloth napkin in hot water, then hold it against the pimple for at least 1 minute.

2 Assess.
Check the pimple. If it has a small white area at the center, it has come to a head: It may be popped to relieve pressure and lessen swelling. If there is no visible head, go to step 4.

3 Pop the pimple.
Place your fingers on either side and gently pull away from the pimple. Do not push inward. The pimple will expel its contents if it is ready, but no harm will be done if it is not.

4 | **Apply cover-up makeup.**
Dab the pimple gently with a tissue to remove any remaining liquid. Apply a cosmetic with a slight green tint to conceal the pimple or the red mark. Red and green are complementary colors and will negate each other, making the pimple less visible.

Rash

1 | **Apply ice.**
If the rash is itchy, place ice in a plastic bag, wrap it in a napkin, and place the bag on the rash. Wait 10 to 15 minutes. The compress will cool any hot patches of skin, numb the area, and reduce any visible swelling.

2 | **If redness and itchiness persist, apply 5 to 10 drops of redness-relieving eye drops to the affected area.**
Spread evenly on the rash with a napkin. The redness should temporarily fade or disappear.

3 | **Cover.**
If any redness remains, apply a small amount of light green, matte eye shadow to the rash. The green will offset the red and make the rash less visible.

4 | **Conceal.**
Depending on the area where the rash is located, it can be strategically covered with short or long dress gloves, a scarf or ascot, hosiery, two strands of pearls, or decorative jewelry glued to the skin.

HOW TO SURVIVE IF THE BRIDE'S GOWN IS LOST

⭐ Make a dress from a tablecloth.

- Remove a white tablecloth from table and cut a hole in the middle.
- Drop it over your head.
- Cut two more holes for your arms.
- Cut around the entire hem of the tablecloth to produce a sash. Tie this around your waist.

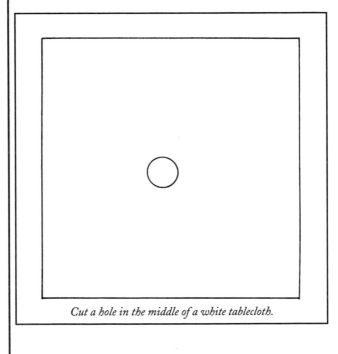

Cut a hole in the middle of a white tablecloth.

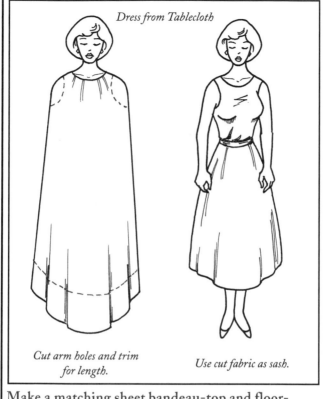

Dress from Tablecloth

Cut arm holes and trim for length.

Use cut fabric as sash.

Make a matching sheet bandeau-top and floor-length skirt.

- Cut a sheet, tablecloth, or curtain into two pieces, with one piece about a third of the cloth and the other the remaining two thirds.
- Tie the smaller piece around your chest and tie it in the back. Adjust the width of your top by folding the fabric to suit before tying and securing. Another option is to bring the fabric from back to

front and make a knot at your sternum. Then twist the remaining fabric to reduce its bulk, bring the ends up and around your neck, and tie a second knot at the nape.

- For your skirt, take the remaining, larger cloth and tie it around your waist, knotting it at the front or side. A side knot will look more demure and bridal. Cut off excess length and quickly baste the bottom seam by bringing a threaded needle up through the fabric, then down and up again, at $1/4$-inch intervals.

✪ Make a sheet ball gown.

- Take an entire sheet and tightly wrap it once around your torso so that the top edge is level with your arm pits. Use safety pins to pin it vertically from the top to mid-thigh to secure it close to your body.

- Wrap the remaining fabric around you again as many times as there is fabric. Pin again vertically where the fabric ends so that the bottom of the sheet rests just above the toes.

- Use scissors to cut a vertical slit from the floor to the back of your knee so you can walk. Baste each edge of the cut fabric so the seams don't fray.

- Pin flowers or decorative appliqué elements taken from hats and handbags onto the dress to hide the safety pins. If anyone asks about your dress, tell them you got it at an exclusive bridal trunk show from a hot new couture designer.

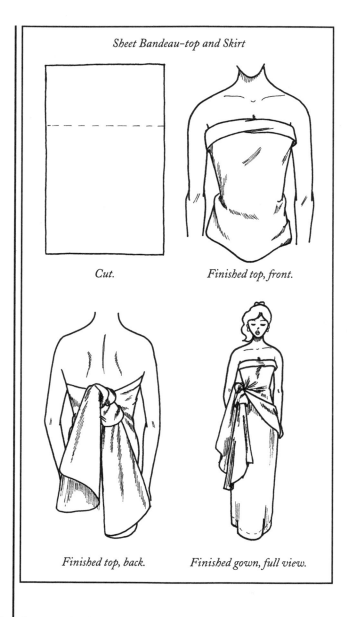

Sheet Bandeau-top and Skirt

Cut.

Finished top, front.

Finished top, back.

Finished gown, full view.

★ Make a tissue paper dress.
  • Scavenge through wedding presents for white wrapping tissue paper.
  • Tape or tuck tissue paper to your underwear or slip to create a floaty, layered look. Use the tissue from several packages for maximum demureness.
  • To give the dress appealing detail, use scissors to make one inch vertical cuts to the tissue paper for fringe.

★ For a more casual or beach wedding, make a kicky, terry-cloth towel dress.
  • Wrap a white towel around your torso.
  • Cut off any overlap and sew the towel together from top to bottom.
  • Safety pin white shoelaces from sneakers or casual shoes to the towel to fashion spaghetti-style straps for your dress.

★ Take a bridesmaid's dress.
  Select the bridesmaid who is closest to you in size. Take her dress and soak it in bleach to make it white. Inform her gently that she is out of the wedding.

HOW TO FIX THE BRIDE'S WEDDING ATTIRE

STAINED DRESS

⭐ For tea, coffee, or dirt stains
- Apply a dot of clear liquid soap and water to a cloth and dab gently on the back of the stain. Do not use excessive water. Do not rub the stain, as you will take the finish off the fibers of the dress.
- Dab the cloth with club soda.
- If the stain remains, dab with a solution of vinegar and water.

⭐ For a red wine stain
- Wet a cloth with white wine and blot behind the stain. Do not rub the stain, as you will take the finish off the fibers of the dress.
- When the stain has faded, dab with water to rinse.

⭐ For grease or makeup stains
- Gently rub a bit of chalk on the stain to absorb the mark. After a few moments, whisk away the chalk dust.
- If you do not have chalk, try baking soda, baby powder, or talcum powder, but they are less absorbent. Sprinkle powder on and then lightly shake off dress.

★ For a lipstick stain
- Dab some petroleum jelly on the mark to dissolve the stain.
- If the stain remains, conceal with baby powder, chalk, or baking powder. Blot the stain to remove as much of it as possible. Pat baby powder on the area gently. Also, try rolling a de-linting brush over the stain to lift it off. This works best for stains that are not embedded into the fibers.

Be Aware
- Before treating a stain, read the label on your dress. The fabric will dictate how or if you should clean it. Silk is the most fragile fabric and toughest to clean. Polyester is the easiest.
- White correction fluid or toothpaste may work to cover up a stain, but because they both possess alcohol, they can pull the color out of your dress, leaving a permanent mark even after professional dry cleaning.
- Avoid using hot water, which will set the stain; always use cool or cold water when cleaning.
- After cleaning a stain, dry the area thoroughly. Water marks are a hazard for dresses, particularly silk ones. Use a hair dryer on the coolest setting to dry the area while stretching the fabric with your fingers to prevent wrinkling.

DRESS WET FROM RAIN

1 Do not put the dress in a clothes dryer.
Dryer heat is too intense and can cause the dress to shrink, wrinkle, and lose beading.

2 Air dry.
Air drying is best when there is just a sprinkling of water on the dress and there is no time left before the ceremony. If you have been caught in a downpour, remove the dress and air dry it, then follow up with some hand steaming to remove the resulting wrinkles. If you do not have a hand steamer, hang the dress in the bathroom while running hot water in the shower, creating a makeshift sauna. Another option is to activate the steam component from a clothes iron and wave it near the dress.

3 Use a hair dryer to dry the dress.
Set the dryer on low and hold it at least 6 inches from the wet fabric. Keep the fabric taut to prevent wrinkling. Use a circular motion with the hair dryer to avoid burning the fabric. Do not try to speed the process by holding the dryer close to the dress; you will only damage the fabric.

4 Use the hot-air dryer in the bathroom.
Do not let the dress drag on the bathroom floor.

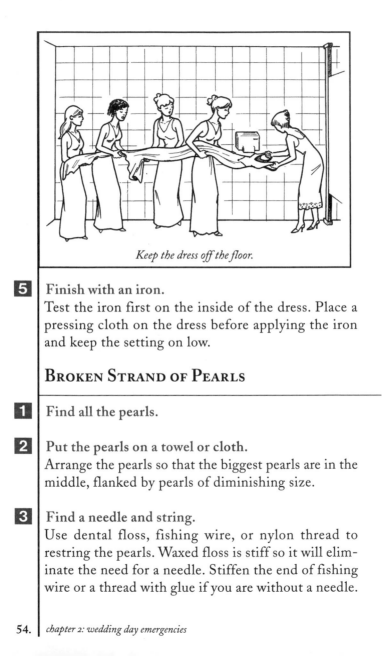

Keep the dress off the floor.

5 Finish with an iron.
Test the iron first on the inside of the dress. Place a pressing cloth on the dress before applying the iron and keep the setting on low.

BROKEN STRAND OF PEARLS

1 Find all the pearls.

2 Put the pearls on a towel or cloth.
Arrange the pearls so that the biggest pearls are in the middle, flanked by pearls of diminishing size.

3 Find a needle and string.
Use dental floss, fishing wire, or nylon thread to restring the pearls. Waxed floss is stiff so it will eliminate the need for a needle. Stiffen the end of fishing wire or a thread with glue if you are without a needle.

4 | Make a triple knot on one end of the string.
Add a dab of glue on top of the knot for extra security. Leave extra length on the string beyond the knot for tying.

5 | Add a pearl.

6 | Make a loose overhand knot.
Place a pin, needle, or tweezers in the open knot and slide the knot next to the pearl. Then pull the knot loop snug as you remove the pin, needle, or tweezers.

7 | Add the next pearl.
Keep your knot-tying tension consistent. If time is running out, tie a knot after every five pearls.

8 | Repeat steps 5 through 7 until all the pearls are on the string.
Make a triple knot after the final pearl. Add a dab of glue to the knot.

9 | Tie the necklace on the bride's neck using a secure square knot.
Dab with glue for added strength. Trim off the excess string.

Be Aware
If the bride's strand of pearls breaks and not enough of the pearls can be located, scan the guests' necks for the best piece of replacement jewelry. Once the most appropriate jewelry has been spotted, ask the

guest to help the bride by lending her the jewels for the big event—or at least for the photographs. Most guests will be flattered to help save the day. Be sure to return the jewelry.

Broken Heel

★ Remove both shoes and go barefoot.
Depending on the length of your dress and the formality of your wedding, going barefoot may be an acceptable option. If you are wearing a floor-length gown, you may need to use straight pins to temporarily hem the dress an inch or two at the bottom to keep it from dragging on the floor and tripping you as you walk.

★ Borrow shoes from others.
Ask a member of the wedding party or a guest with the same size foot if you can wear her shoes for the ceremony. Do not be choosy about style or color.

★ Make an emergency heel.
Find a sturdy object or objects the same height as the broken heel. A shot glass, a stack of sticky notes (so long as it's not raining), or a votive candleholder are acceptable choices. Alternatively, use duct tape to make a cylinder out of several short pencils or metal lipstick tubes. Wrap duct tape around your shoe and the substitute heel to secure it in place.

Locate available options.

Secure replacement heel to shoe.

Do not walk more than ten yards.

Be Aware

- A replacement heel is fine for a short period of light activity, but do not dance, run, carry heavy objects, walk more than 10 yards, or stand for long periods of time with your weight on the emergency heel.

- Once the dancing begins at the reception, your guests will be relieved to see that you have removed your shoes. They will feel much more comfortable about taking off their own uncomfortable and restricting shoes and having fun.

EMERGENCY UP-DO HAIRSTYLE

1 Brush your hair back from your forehead.
Comb it long enough to make the hair on top of your head smooth.

2 Gather your hair at the nape, slightly to the left, as if you were going to put in a low ponytail.

3 Twist the hair twice, in a clockwise direction, to anchor it in place.
You can also use bobby pins to hold the hair in place.

4 Brush the remaining hair down toward the direction of the nape of your neck.

5 Twist it clockwise while lifting the ends.
You are creating a roll effect on the back of your head.

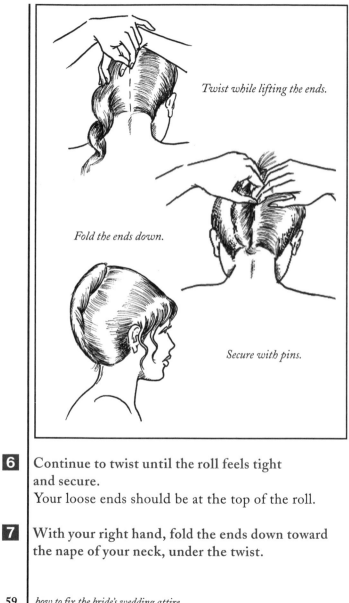

Twist while lifting the ends.

Fold the ends down.

Secure with pins.

6 Continue to twist until the roll feels tight and secure.
Your loose ends should be at the top of the roll.

7 With your right hand, fold the ends down toward the nape of your neck, under the twist.

8 | Pin the roll in place.
Use your left hand to hold the twist in place while your right hand works the bobby pins. Slide one long pin in the top of the roll, facing down. Place another long pin in the bottom, going up the middle. Insert a final large pin at an angle through the side of the roll. Finish with enough small bobby pins to secure the twist and smooth any ruffled areas.

9 | Pull out a few tendrils.
Loosen a few strands of hair around your face for a more romantic look. Curl the strands with a curling iron if one is available.

10 | Spray the twist in place with hairspray.

HOW TO FIX THE GROOM'S WEDDING ATTIRE

Tux Too Small

 Swap tuxedos.
If your tuxedo matches the style of those worn by the groomsmen or waiter, exchange yours for one that fits: It is better for a groomsman or waiter to look poorly dressed than the groom.

 Expand the waistband.
Make a chain of two or three safety pins, depending on how much additional room is required. Secure the sides of the waistband together using pins. Your cummerbund will hide the fix. Do not remove the cummerbund during the wedding.

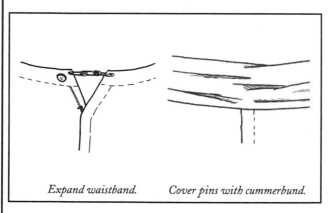

Expand waistband.　　　*Cover pins with cummerbund.*

★ Replace the pants.
Locate a pair of black pants that fit. Cut a piece of black electrical tape the same length as the pant leg, waist to hem. Cut the tape in half lengthwise. Affix one half on the side seam of the right leg of the pants. Repeat for your left leg.

★ Keep the jacket unbuttoned.
Buttoning the jacket will make the improper fit more apparent.

★ Distract with your cufflinks.
If the jacket sleeves are too short, make sure your cufflinks are of a high quality. Keep your arms slightly bent at all times to reduce the obviousness of the length disparity.

★ Expand the shirt collar.
Loop a rubber band through the buttonhole of the shirt collar. Secure the ends to the collar button. Conceal with a necktie. Do not remove the tie during the wedding.

Split Seam

1 Remove the jacket, shirt, or pants.

2 Turn the garment inside out.

3 Pull the seam together.
There will be a narrow section of fabric behind the

seam. Pull the split sections together. Line up the sides carefully.

4 Pin.
Using safety pins, connect the two sides. Pin the material as close to the seam as possible, but not so close that the pins will be visible from the outside.

5 Check the repair.
Turn the garment right-side out. If the seam holds and the pins are not visible, the repair was successful. If the pins are visible, remove and start over.

Be Aware
If no safety pins are available, use staples. Take care when removing them to prevent rips in the fabric. If neither pins nor staples are available, use electrical or duct tape. Fast-drying glue is also effective for repairing torn garments, but may damage or stain the fabric.

LOST BOW TIE

Make an emergency replacement from a cloth napkin.
- Place a well-starched white dinner napkin flat on a table in front of you. Using a pencil, carefully draw a circle about 1 inch in diameter.
- To the left of the circle, draw a triangle with sides about 2 inches long. One point of the triangle should extend slightly into the circle.

• Repeat, drawing a second triangle to the right of the circle, with one point extending into the circle. Your drawing should look like a bow tie when viewed from the front.

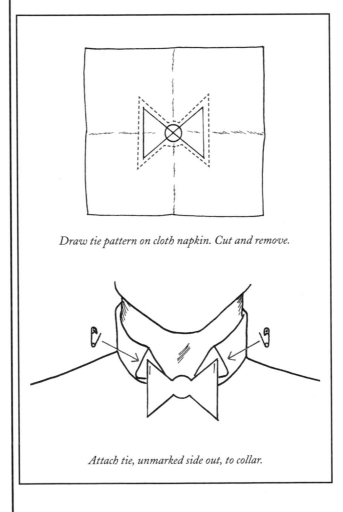

Draw tie pattern on cloth napkin. Cut and remove.

Attach tie, unmarked side out, to collar.

- Use scissors to cut the bow tie from the napkin. Turn the bow tie over so the pencil marks are on the back.
- Secure the cutout to your collar using loops of tape or safety pins. Do not wear with a black cummerbund: Make an emergency napkin cummerbund (see page 68) to match.

✪ Wear a medallion.

Open your shirt at the collar and open three additional buttons. For a more fashionable look, borrow a spread collar shirt (one without a wing collar, which is made for a bow tie). Borrow and wear a large medallion, gold cross, Star of David, giant locket, or flashy pendant. To make a medallion:

- Open a wedding gift wrapped in gold-colored wrapping paper.
- Wrap the gold paper around a drink coaster or a similar-sized piece of cardboard. Cut the paper to fit, then tape or glue to cover.
- Affix your medallion to a black dress shoelace or piece of string with tape.
- Hang around your neck.

✪ Make a bolo tie.
- Thread a black shoelace (leather or nylon) under and around your shirt collar to simulate a bolo lanyard.
- Run the two loose ends through the backing of a pin, pendant, or horizontal tie clasp.
- Slide the clasp up so it sits just below the second shirt button. Keep your collar button open.

EMERGENCY CUFF LINKS

1 Remove your shirt.

2 Thread a narrow ($1/8$- to -inch-wide) ribbon through the cuff holes.
Leave the cuff open about half an inch. Do not tie the ends.

3 Tie knots.
On the outside of one cuff, tie a small knot on the ribbon as close to the hole as possible. Tie a second knot on top of the first.

4 Check the knot diameter.
Test the knot by pulling gently on the other end of the ribbon. If the knot pulls through easily, tie another knot on top of the first two.

5 Trim the ends.
When the knot is too big to fit through the hole easily, snip the excess ribbon just past the knot. Repeat on the other side of the cuff, then on the other sleeve. The knots may be pushed through the cuff holes after the shirt is on. They will hold the cuffs closed and look similar to braided silk cuff knots.

Be Aware

• Keep the jacket sleeve pulled down as far as possible to hide an unsightly fix.

Emergency Cuff Links

shoelace

cherry stem

twist tie

- Items that can be used as emergency cuff links:
  - paper clips
  - twist ties
  - rubber bands
  - the metal rings from two key chains
  - large earrings
  - Maraschino cherry stems tied in knots
  - shoelaces (cut short)

Emergency Cummerbund

You will need a white cloth napkin for a white-tie wedding or a black or dark blue napkin for a black-tie event, plus a couple additional napkins to secure the cummerbund. The napkins should be starched and slightly stiff.

1 Place the napkin flat on a table in front of you, with one corner pointing toward you.

2 Fold the corner closest to you and the opposite corner into the center of the napkin.

3 Fold the bottom half of the napkin up toward the top edge.
The bottom edge should be about one inch above the top edge when the fold is complete.

4 Fold both upper edges down toward the bottom edge. The lower of the two pleats should be one inch above the bottom edge. The napkin should now have three pleats and be the approximate shape of a cummer-bund.

5 Secure.
Tightly roll another napkin on the diagonal so it is long and thin. Tie or pin the second (or two more) napkin(s) to one end of the cummerbund, run it around your back, then tie or pin it to the other end. The pleats of the cummerbund should face up. Your jacket will obscure the sides of the napkin, even when unbuttoned.

PREVENT PERSPIRATION STAINS FROM SHOWING

✪ Wear an undershirt.
A thin cotton T-shirt will absorb sweat before it reaches your exterior layer of clothing.

✪ Wear perspiration shields.
Tape several layers of tissue paper, paper towels, or cocktail napkins to the underarm area of your shirt to absorb excess wetness. Do not use colored tissue or napkins because the ink from the dye may stain your shirt when wet.

✪ Wear chamois.
Cut a piece of chamois cloth, the ultra-absorbent cloth often employed for drying and polishing cars, into two 4-inch squares. Tape the squares to the underarm area of your shirt to remain extra dry.

⭐ Wear a pantiliner.

Apply a self-sticking pantiliner or other feminine product to the underarm area of the shirt. Make sure you remove the product in private before joining your new spouse after the wedding.

Be Aware

If you discover that the sweat has come through and is visible on your shirt, use a blow-dryer or hot-air hand dryer to dry the wet areas. It is not necessary to remove the shirt first.

HOW TO DEAL WITH WEDDING-RELATED INJURIES

CAN'T FIT RING ON FINGER

⭐ Try the other hand.
The ring finger on the opposite hand may naturally be slightly smaller in diameter.

⭐ Try a different finger.
No one will notice if, for a little while, the ring is on the pinky.

⭐ Elevate hand.
Hands and feet swell in warm, humid weather. Hold your arm above your head for several minutes. Blood will flow from the hand and reduce the swelling so the ring will fit.

⭐ Grease finger.
Coat the ring finger with lip gloss, petroleum jelly, butter, margarine, or water.

⭐ Cool finger.
Submerge your ring finger in a glass of ice water for 15 minutes. The cold will constrict blood vessels and shrink the diameter of the finger slightly.

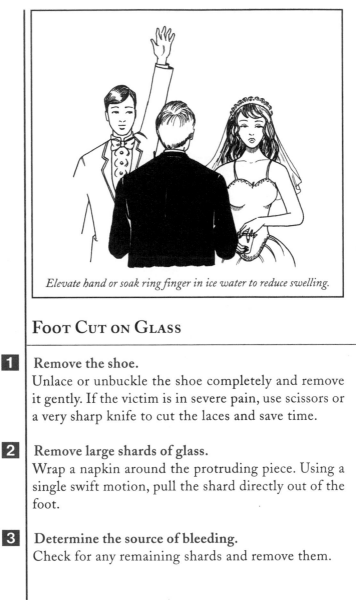

Elevate hand or soak ring finger in ice water to reduce swelling.

Foot Cut on Glass

1 Remove the shoe.
Unlace or unbuckle the shoe completely and remove it gently. If the victim is in severe pain, use scissors or a very sharp knife to cut the laces and save time.

2 Remove large shards of glass.
Wrap a napkin around the protruding piece. Using a single swift motion, pull the shard directly out of the foot.

3 Determine the source of bleeding.
Check for any remaining shards and remove them.

4 | Stop the bleeding.
Using towels, napkins, or tablecloths, apply direct pressure to the wound for 5 minutes. If the wound is spurting, sustain pressure for 15 minutes.

5 | Clean the foot.
Soak the foot in a bowl filled with warm water, then use a damp napkin or clean sponge to gently rub off any remaining blood.

6 | Inspect the wound.
Using your fingers, gently spread the sides of the wound apart. Look closely for any remaining glass shards. Remove with sterile tweezers (hold the tweezers under hot running water for 30 seconds, then in a candle flame for 30 seconds). The wound should stop bleeding profusely when all the glass has been removed.

7 | Treat and bandage.
Apply a thin layer of antibiotic ointment to the wound. Cover with a sterile adhesive bandage or gauze and medical tape.

Be Aware

• Wounds through the sole of the shoe may become infected by the microbe *Pseudomonas*.
• Wounds $1/2$ inch in length or longer should be sutured at a hospital.
• If the victim has not had a tetanus booster in the last five years, one should be given at a hospital within 48 hours of the injury.

- Seeping from the injury site may indicate that glass remains in the wound.
- When wrapping a glass in a napkin for the Jewish wedding ritual, be sure to lay the glass on its side before stomping on it.

FALL FROM CHAIR DURING CHAIR DANCE

1 Seat the victim.

If the victim is conscious, move her to a chair and have her sit down. If she is unconscious on the floor, leave her in place. Most people who are knocked out after a fall regain consciousness within a few minutes.

2 Test cognition.

Ask the victim her name. Have her point to a few family members or friends in attendance and state their names. Ask her what type of event she is attending and the city in which it is being held. Ask her to state the date, including the day of the week and year. Correct answers indicate that she has not suffered a concussion. If she answers incorrectly, check again in 10 minutes.

3 Check responsiveness.

Ask the victim to follow your finger with her eyes as you move it from side to side and up and down. Ask her to move her arms and legs in coordinated motions. Help the victim stand, then ask her to walk forward, then backward, then forward again. Accomplishing these tasks indicates there is no neurological damage.

4 Watch for vomiting or loss of consciousness.
Pay particular attention to the victim for the next hour.

5 Prevent alcohol consumption.
Ask the victim if she has had anything alcoholic to drink or has taken tranquilizers or other medication, all of which may mimic the symptoms of injury. Do not let the victim drink.

Chapped Lips from Kissing

✪ Apply lip balm.
Spread a thin layer of petroleum jelly, vitamin E, or skin cream (used sparingly) to lips. Wait several minutes for the treatment to be absorbed.

✪ Apply olive oil.
Using your fingers, work a small amount of olive oil into your lips. Wait several minutes for the lips to become less slippery.

✪ Apply butter.
Work butter into your lips using your fingers. To prevent infection, avoid using butter if your lips are cracked and bleeding.

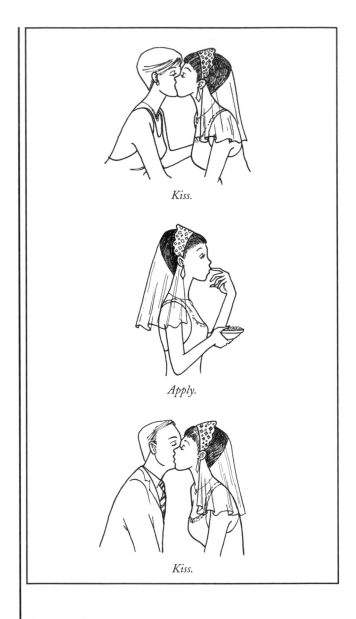

Kiss.

Apply.

Kiss.

HIT IN THE EYE WITH BOUQUET

1 Check the eye for swelling.
If the eyelid is swollen shut and covering the eyeball, reduce the swelling before continuing with treatment. Place a handful of ice in a cloth napkin and twist it closed. Wrap it in a second napkin and place it on the injured eye for 15 minutes, removing it occasionally to check swelling.

2 Examine the cornea.
Under a bright overhead light or pointing a flashlight at the injured eye, instruct the victim to look in all directions and blink repeatedly. Carefully examine the sclera (the white of the eye) and the cornea (the layer covering the pupil and iris) for any foreign material: petal shards, pieces of stem, or leaves.

3 Assemble irrigation equipment.
Obtain a clean, unused liquor spout from the bartender. Place the pourer on a bottle of flat spring water or a bottle filled with cool tap water.

4 Irrigate the cornea.
With the victim seated and her head tilted so she is looking up at the ceiling, gently push her eyelids back and away from the cornea using your thumb and forefinger. From a low height, delicately pour a steady stream of cool water on the eyeball. Occasionally wipe the area around the eye socket with a clean napkin.

5 | Check the eye.
After a full bottle has been poured, dry the area and check the eyeball for remaining foreign material. If any material is still present, repeat irrigation with a second bottle of water.

6 | Check for corneal abrasion.
Instruct the victim to look in all directions and blink repeatedly for several seconds. If she reports blurred vision, discomfort, or notes a sensation of something in her eye, a corneal abrasion may be present. Seek medical attention immediately.

SPRAINED ANKLE

1 | Prepare a cold compress.
Place ice in a plastic bag. Wrap the bag in a piece of clothing, or place it in a second plastic bag.

2 | Elevate the ankle.
Seat the victim and raise the injured ankle at least 18 inches from the ground; a chair works well. Keep the ankle in this position.

3 | Hold the compress on the ankle.
The cold will constrict blood vessels and reduce swelling.

4 | Leave the compress in place for 30 minutes.
If the sprain is particularly bad and swelling is rapid and severe, leave the compress on for 15 additional minutes.

5 | Test the ankle.
Have the victim put weight on the injured ankle. If standing or walking is still too painful, continue to step 6.

6 | Construct a pressure bandage.
Cut or tear a tablecloth, shirt, or another piece of material into two 3-foot-long, 4-inch-wide strips.

7 | Wrap the ankle.
Place one end of the bandage in the middle of the foot. Using a figure-8 pattern, bring the cloth up and over the ankle and back around the foot. The bandage should be snug and the ankle immobile. Use rubber bands, a garter, or two bow ties to secure the bandage to the leg.

8 | Administer pain medication.
Ibuprofen will reduce swelling and relieve pain. If ibuprofen is not available, offer acetaminophen or aspirin.

9 | Limit dancing.

HOW TO DEAL WITH OUTDOOR WEDDING DISASTERS

⭐ Extreme heat
- Have the caterer serve all refrigerated items immediately. Do not be concerned about mixing up traditional courses such as dessert, dinner, and appetizers. Serve ice cream and fish first and save bread, crackers, and other nonperishables for last.
- Soak napkins in ice water and wear as headbands, neck wraps, or hats.
- Remove nonessential clothing.

⭐ Extreme cold
- Tell guests to huddle together to use body heat to stay warm. Cram additional guests into each row of seats or table. Place children on laps of adults for additional heat source.
- Pass out candles in glass globes. Guests can hold the globe as a hand warmer, passing it along after a few moments.

⭐ Rain with no tent
- Make a paper hat. Take a wedding program and orient it in front of you as you would to read it. Turn it 90 degrees so that the bound part is on top and the open part is on the bottom. Take the top

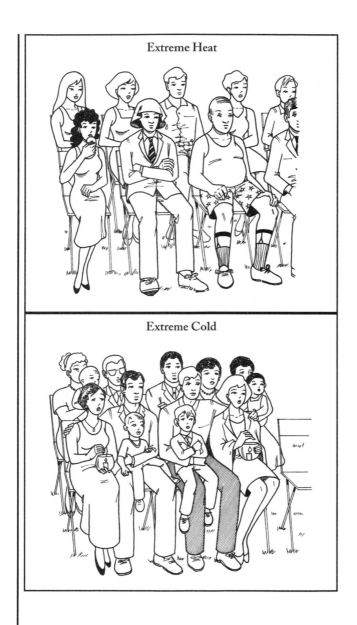

Extreme Heat

Extreme Cold

how to deal with outdoor wedding disasters

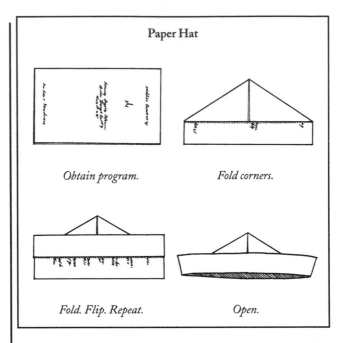

Paper Hat

Obtain program.

Fold corners.

Fold. Flip. Repeat.

Open.

two corners of the program and fold them into the middle. Now take the bottom flap and fold up once or twice. Turn "hat" over and turn up the other page once or twice. You now have a "Napoleon" style paper hat. Perch it delicately on your head to keep the water off your face.

- Have the groomsmen pick up the aisle runner and hold it over the heads of the bride, groom, and officiant as a canopy.
- Instruct guests to take off their jackets and hold them over their heads as makeshift umbrellas.

★ Swarm of insects

- Grind up garlic, mix with water, and spray flying insects to repel them. Kill mosquitoes by spraying them with catnip oil. To stop invasions of ants, grind citrus peels and mix with water, then dump on hill.

- Instruct guests or members of the wedding party wearing yellow to change the color of their clothes. Likewise, guests wearing citrus-infused perfumes and colognes should wash them off. Bumblebees are attracted to the color yellow and the odor of citrus.

- Build a yellow-jacket trap. Find a two-liter bottle and cut off the top several inches. Invert the top and place it into the bottle. Staple the pieces together for added security. Find a sweet-smelling liquid (orange soda, vanilla soda, root beer, lemonade) and pour five ounces into the bottle as a lure. The yellow jackets will fly in but won't be able to escape.

- Place sweet-smelling strips of fabric softener on tables to repel insects.

Be Aware

If you are not completely comfortable with the possibility of storms, infestations, floods, and other extreme weather, plan an indoor wedding.

HOW TO AVOID AN ALLERGIC REACTION TO FLOWERS

1 **Be alert to the smell of flowers.**
Highly fragrant flowers (including roses and lilies) are likely to have open buds, more pollen, and a higher level of allergy danger.

2 **Send an usher or bridesmaid to examine the buds.**
Floral buds that are completely open—especially flowers that are dying—release more pollen, which causes allergic reactions. If buds are wide open, do not approach the flower.

3 **Ask the attendant to check the interior of the bud.**
Pollen is supplied by the stamen, the male reproductive organ in a flower. The stamen usually consists of a long filament topped by an anther, which holds the pollen. If the stamen is highly visible, the flower is more likely to cause an allergic reaction.

4 **Instruct the attendant to clip the anthers.**
Using a sharp pair of scissors, carefully cut all the anthers and remove.

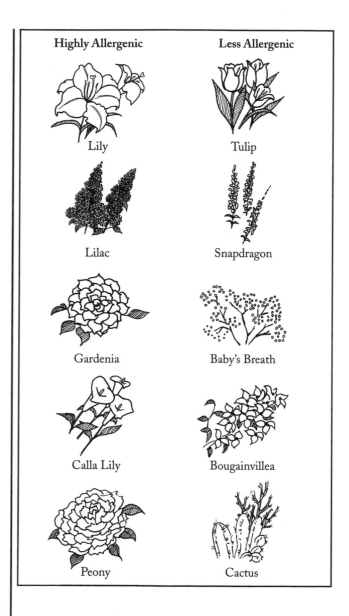

Highly Allergenic

Lily

Lilac

Gardenia

Calla Lily

Peony

Less Allergenic

Tulip

Snapdragon

Baby's Breath

Bougainvillea

Cactus

how to avoid an allergic reaction to flowers

5 Avoid sap.

Floral sap can cause severe allergic reactions. The clear sap from lily stems causes "lily rash," a persistent itch that may come and go for years. Do not touch sap or place your hands in water that has been in contact with lilies. Avoid the milky white sap, called latex, from poinsettias, cacti, and other *Euphorbias*: It is highly allergenic and can cause blindness if rubbed in the eyes.

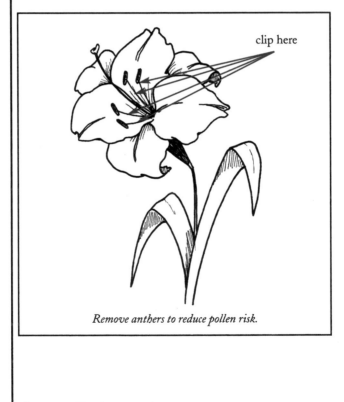

clip here

Remove anthers to reduce pollen risk.

CEREMONY SURVIVAL SKILLS

HOW TO SURVIVE IF THE FLOWERS DON'T ARRIVE

★ Use fruit.
Stack seasonal fruits in glass vases: cherries and navel oranges for spring weddings, strawberries and blueberries for summer, apples for autumn, or holly and pinecones for winter.

★ Borrow flowers.
Good hotels will have beautiful, ornate floral arrangements in the lobby area, in public spaces and sitting areas, and in the bar/restaurant. Dressed in your wedding attire, approach the manager to explain your situation. Tip generously.

★ Borrow from another wedding in the hotel or reception hall.
Ask someone in the other wedding party if you can use flowers from that wedding. Do not be choosey—don't decline some arrangements because the colors are wrong or you don't like them—and don't approach the bride and groom, since they probably will be busy.

★ Knock on neighbors' doors.
Explain your situation to people in nearby houses. Ask to borrow flowers from their gardens and construct bouquets and small arrangements.

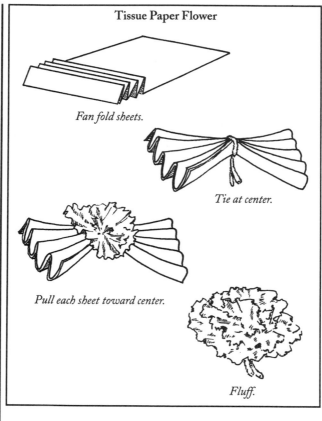

Tissue Paper Flower

Fan fold sheets.

Tie at center.

Pull each sheet toward center.

Fluff.

✪ Make flowers from tissue paper.

- Stack three sheets of 6-x-12-inch tissue paper. Each piece should be a different color. If you don't have tissue paper on hand, open a few gifts—most will include tissue paper in the box.

- Make a 1-inch-wide fold up from the bottom (shorter) edge of the pile, then continue fan folding the sheets to the top edge.

- Fold a pipe cleaner or twist tie in half. Place the tissue paper inside the fold of the twist tie, then twist the ends together just under the sheets. The pipe cleaner or twist tie will act as the stem of the flower (you may need two twist ties to achieve the proper length).
- Fan the tissue pieces out, then carefully pull up each crease, starting with the top layer and continuing with the next two to form the petals of the flower. Fluff the paper to add volume.
- Repeat.

★ Borrow from a nearby cemetery.

Scout out graves with very large headstones, monuments, or other elaborate markers, which are likely to have more impressive arrangements. Find a fresh arrangement at a location with no one around. Before taking the flowers, take careful note of the grave's location so that you can return them after the wedding.

Be Aware

- If the flowers are severely drooping or nearly dead, re-cut the stems and place them in cool water. Make a 45-degree cut at least an inch from the bottom of the stems and remove all leaves and thorns below the water level. Add half a teaspoon of sugar to the vase to keep the flowers fresh; use lemon-lime or other clear soda if sugar is not available. Do not use cola. Then use a well-shaken bottle of sparkling water to spray the petals and

leaves with water. Avoid club soda, which contains sodium.
• Virtually all flowers dislike drafts, whether hot or cold. Keep arrangements away from doors, open windows, air conditioning and heating vents, and radiators.

How to Make an Emergency Bouquet

You will need 5 long pencils or pens, invisible tape, 5 colorful neckties, scissors, and curling ribbon from several large wedding presents.

1 Prepare a pencil or pen.
Wrap a piece of tape around the eraser-side of each pencil, with the sticky-side of the tape facing out. Secure the tape in place with another piece of tape so it will stay at the top of the pencil.

2 Roll a necktie into a rosette.
Affix the skinny end of the tie to the sticky tape at the end of the pencil. Tightly roll the tie over on itself, around the pencil, forming a tie rosette. As you continue to roll toward the thicker end of the tie, be sure to keep the top edge straight so the spirals create a rosette.

3 Secure the end with tape.
When you've run out of fabric, secure the end of the tie in place with a piece of tape.

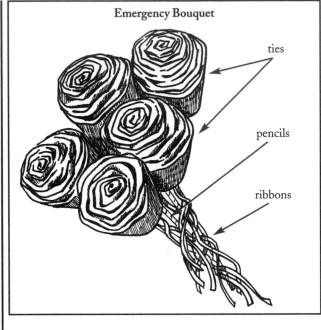

Emergency Bouquet

ties

pencils

ribbons

4 Repeat steps 1 through 3 with the remaining pencils and ties.

5 Tie the "flowers" together with ribbon.
Construct a bouquet by fashioning all of the tie rosettes into a makeshift bouquet. Wrap the pencils with several long strands of curling ribbon and tie a knot to hold them together. Allow some of the curly ribbon to hang low for a pretty effect.

Be Aware
For a more demure bouquet, cut the ties in half for smaller rosettes.

HOW TO SURVIVE IF THE OFFICIANT DOESN'T SHOW UP

⭐ **Call for a substitute.**
Inquire at other rectories and churches for an available officiant.

⭐ **Inquire among guests if there is a judge or person "of the cloth" in the house.**

⭐ **Ordain a friend.**
Select someone who has a flair for drama and is comfortable with public speaking. Visit the Universal Life Church Website (www.ulc.org) or the Spiritual Humanist Website (www.spiritualhumanism.org). Instantly ordain your friend as a minister.

⭐ **Use an impostor.**
Select a wedding guest or passerby who looks the part of your officiant. Have him or her perform the ceremony. After the reception, complete a civil ceremony to make your union official.

Be Aware
Sea captains only have the authority to perform marriages on board a ship at sea.

HOW TO TREAT
A PANIC ATTACK

1 Realize that you're panicking.
Panic begets panic. Do not panic about panicking.
Tell yourself that you are not dying or going crazy, but
experiencing an anxiety attack. This awareness will
prevent the attack from escalating.

2 Loosen your clothes.
Do not tear off your dress or jacket. Open a few buttons; lower a zipper.

3 Control your breathing.
Prevent hyperventilation by slowing your breathing.
Breathe into a paper bag to restore a balance of oxy-
gen and carbon dioxide in your lungs.

4 Distract yourself.
Focus on a physical object in the room. While breathing into the bag, close your eyes and try to recall the
location and colors of all the objects in the room.

5 Act natural.
Open your eyes. Stop using the bag. Refasten zippers
and buttons. Walk. Try to smile. Tell yourself it's over
and everything is fine.

6 Resume your activities.

Control your breathing.

Be Aware

- An attack usually lasts between 15 and 30 minutes. Symptoms include pounding heart, sweating, dilated pupils, trembling, dry mouth, shortness of breath or sensation of being smothered, feelings of being choked, chest pain, nausea, dizziness, sense of being detached from oneself, and fear of losing control or going crazy.
- Knowing that you can conquer the attacks will sharply reduce their occurrence. Conversely, knowing that you are prey to attacks and cannot control them may sharply increase their occurrence.

How to Avoid a Nervous Breakdown Before the Wedding

⭐ **Ignore minor irritations.**
Avoid driving at rush hour, upgrading your computer software, dealing with a governmental agency, thinking about your job, rooting for any sports team, undertaking a plumbing project, or listening to the local news.

⭐ **Imagine yourself in a relaxing situation.**
As you visualize, hold onto something tactile—a lucky rabbit's foot or your grandmother's favorite handkerchief. Hold it again later to restore your sense of calm. If you do not have a soothing object when the panic begins, conjure up safe and peaceful images.

⭐ **Practice yoga.**
Find a quiet room and close door. Dim the lights.
- Tree pose. Stand with your feet together. Draw your left foot up your right leg until it rests on your inner thigh. Put the palms of your hands together and raise them over your head. Balance and remain still. Lower your leg and repeat with the other side.
- Child's pose. Get on your hands and knees and sit back so that your bottom touches your heels and your chest is resting on your thighs. Keep your arms alongside your body with your fingers close to your ankles and your cheek on the floor. Rest.
- Corpse pose. Remain on the floor. Turn over on

Stress-Reducing Yoga Poses

tree pose   child's pose

your back. Rest your arms and legs flat on the floor. Close your eyes and relax every muscle. Do this for as long as it takes, but for at least 5 minutes. Do not fall asleep. Get up slowly when you feel calm, or when it is time to walk down the aisle.

✪ Laugh.
Rent videos of musicals from the 1930s, 1940s, and 1950s, especially those with Gene Kelly and Fred Astaire.

Go to sleep early the night before the wedding.
Even if you cannot sleep, at least your body will be resting. Do not plan the bachelor or bachelorette party for the night before the ceremony.

 Eat and drink.
Make sure you eat on the big day, even if you do not feel hungry. Avoid caffeine, alcohol, and gassy, bloating foods. Remain hydrated. If you are prone to fainting, drink some juice, sugary soda, or a shot of grappa (for courage) before walking down the aisle.

 Elope.

Be Aware
If something goes wrong, keep in mind that it will make for a hilarious story at anniversary parties.

HOW TO FIND THE GROOM

1   Be patient.
The groom will probably be back in a minute.

2   Locate the best man.
The best man should know the groom's whereabouts at all times. If he does not, enlist his help in the search. If both the groom and the best man are missing, seek help from the ushers or the groom's parents and siblings.

3   Establish communication procedures.
Equip all members of the search party with mobile phones. Exchange numbers and set up a phone tree. Alternatively, set up a conference call and stay on the line.

4   Split up.
You will cover more ground more quickly with multiple people searching independently.

5   Check the bathroom.
The groom may be adjusting his attire, mopping his brow, or dealing with a nervous stomach.

6   Check the front and rear entrances of the building.
The groom may be getting some air to calm his nerves.

Where Is the Groom?

chapter 3: ceremony survival skills

7 Check the water cooler.

Look for vending machines and a water fountain. The groom may be having a glass of water to cool off.

8 Check the parking lot.

See if the car the groom arrived in is still there.

9 Check nearby bars.

10 Check the bus depot, train station, and airport.

Be Aware

- Do not approach guests and ask if they have seen the groom. This will be awkward, at best.
- After the groom has been missing for two hours, announce to guests that there has been a change in scheduling.

How to Stall the Ceremony

1 Keep music playing.

2 Announce a short delay.

The best man or maid of honor should deliver the message: "Sorry, we are running a little late. We will let you know when we are ready to begin."

3 Serve food and alcohol.

If the ceremony and reception are happening in the same place, instruct the caterer to pass cold hors d'oeuvres and glasses of champagne.

4 Stay out of sight.
The bride should not mingle with the guests while the hunt for the groom continues. With neither the bride nor the groom present, guests will not become as suspicious.

5 Show photo albums/videos of the happy couple.

6 Ask if anyone else wants to get married.
A spontaneous wedding is a memorable opening act, and doesn't increase the costs.

HOW TO DEAL WITH AN INTOXICATED BRIDESMAID

1 Remove her shoes.

Do not expect the intoxicated bridesmaid to walk down the aisle wearing high heels.

2 Have all the bridesmaids line up in pairs.

Couple the intoxicated bridesmaid with another member of the wedding party who is strong enough to support her weight.

3 Help her down the aisle.

Position the intoxicated bridesmaid to the right of her partner. The partner should put her right arm around the bridesmaid's waist, with her left hand firmly grasping the intoxicated bridesmaid's left forearm so she can provide support and guide her down the aisle. The intoxicated bridesmaid should carry both of their bouquets in her left hand to hide the support.

4 Ask the musicians to play the processional music at a slower tempo.

The slower pace will help the intoxicated bridesmaid to keep her balance as she walks in time to the music.

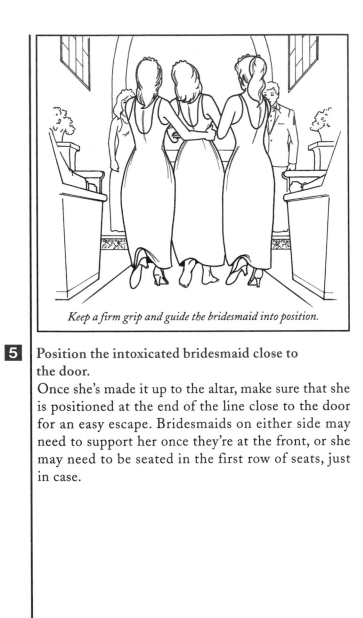

Keep a firm grip and guide the bridesmaid into position.

5 Position the intoxicated bridesmaid close to the door.

Once she's made it up to the altar, make sure that she is positioned at the end of the line close to the door for an easy escape. Bridesmaids on either side may need to support her once they're at the front, or she may need to be seated in the first row of seats, just in case.

HOW TO MAINTAIN COMPOSURE DURING THE CEREMONY

CRYING JAG

⭐ **Take deep, measured breaths.**
Inhale through your nose and exhale through your mouth. Deep breathing will calm you and prevent hyperventilation brought on by crying.

⭐ **Stare at inanimate objects.**
Focus on floral arrangements, your clothing, or the floor.

⭐ **Recall trivial details.**
Try to remember the color of your childhood blanket, or the make and model of all the cars you have owned. Attempt to say the alphabet or the months of the year backward.

⭐ **Stand up straight.**
Crying will cause you to bend forward and make your head and shoulders shake. Concentrate on good posture: Keep your back straight and your head held high to combat the physical effects of your emotions.

Be Aware
Crying at weddings tends to be contagious and mutually reinforcing. Do not look at others who are crying or you may lose control.

Laughing Fit

★ Bite your tongue.
Bite down on your tongue hard enough to cause pain but not so hard that you cause bleeding or other injury.

★ Prick your finger.
Using the pin from your boutonniere or a thorn from a rose in your bouquet, quickly stick the pad of your thumb to cause pain. Put pressure on the pricked area for several minutes to avoid bloodstained clothing.

★ Pinch yourself.
The skin on the back of the upper arm is very sensitive. Squeeze a small section of skin between the thumb and index finger of your opposite hand. Release quickly to avoid a bruise.

★ Think about how much the wedding costs.

Hiccups

1 Inhale through your mouth.

2 Hold your breath.

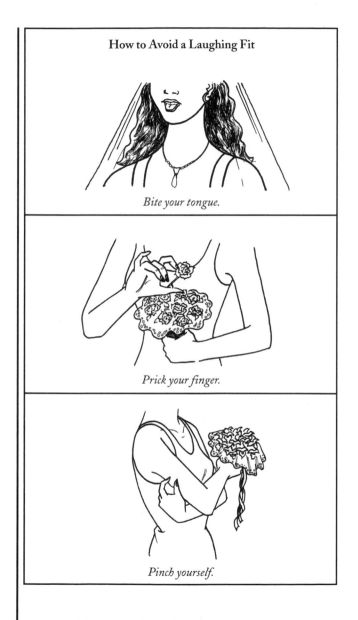

How to Avoid a Laughing Fit

Bite your tongue.

Prick your finger.

Pinch yourself.

3 | Slowly count to ten.

4 | Swallow three times slowly.

5 | Exhale.

6 | Repeat.

Standing on your head while drinking backward from a glass will not cure hiccups.

Be Aware

Swallow a flat (nonheaping) teaspoon or one paper packet of sugar in one quick gulp. Do not use a sugar substitute. Do not use salt.

FLATULENCE

 Alter your stance.
Flatulence is more audible with the legs and buttocks close together. Shift your position so your feet are approximately 3 feet apart.

 Sit down.

 Shift the blame.
Look disapprovingly at a nearby guest or member of the bridal party. Do not look accusingly at your betrothed.

Be Aware

• Avoid introducing excess gas into your system. Do not smoke, chew gum, or drink carbonated beverages, and avoid beans, broccoli, cabbage, cauliflower, onions, and dairy products (if lactose intolerant) just before the ceremony.

• Chew activated charcoal tablets before the wedding. The charcoal will absorb odor caused by intestinal bacteria. Do not chew briquettes.

HOW TO SURVIVE IF SOMEONE OBJECTS

1 Laugh it off.
Smile, laugh, and keep things moving.

2 Make a joke.
If the protester persists, loudly exclaim, "Mom, it's going to be all right," or "I thought we were serving the liquor after the ceremony!"

3 Turn the crowd against the protester.
Say "This is the most important day of our lives, and we ask that you honor it with us."

4 Direct the best man to handle it.
If the guest continues to object, the best man should approach her, tell her quietly that she is disrupting the ceremony, and escort her out or to a side room, giving her the attention she craves.

5 Consider the objection in private.
If the protester might have a legitimate objection (the groom is currently married to her), the best man should tell the bride, groom, and officiant, who should all discuss the matter before the ceremony continues.

Be Aware
The consent of guests is not required for the marriage ceremony to be completed.

HOW TO DEAL WITH LOST RINGS

★ Use cigar bands.
The best man or groomsmen may have cigars in their pockets. Slip the paper band off the cigar and give one to the bride and one to the groom to use in place of wedding bands. Large cigars with wide ring gauges have bands that are most likely to fit.

★ Borrow from guests.
Send the best man to collect rings from guests. Ask him to bring back an assortment of sizes so that one is sure to fit. The style of the ring does not matter.

★ Use a ponytail holder.
Twist the elastic in figure-8s until it is small enough to fit on a finger.

★ Bend paperclips.
Straighten and then bend the paperclips into a ring. Watch for sharp ends.

★ Braid rubber bands.
Braid three rubber bands, then tie loose ends together to form a ring.

How to Make an Emergency Ring

You will need the foil wrapper from a stick of chewing gum and a piece of tape. For a man's ring, use an entire wrapper; for a woman's ring, use a wrapper that has been cut in half lengthwise.

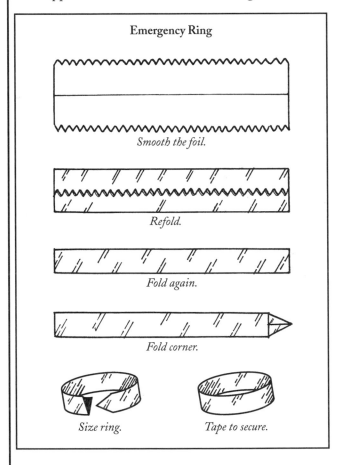

Emergency Ring

Smooth the foil.

Refold.

Fold again.

Fold corner.

Size ring.

Tape to secure.

1 | Remove the gum from the foil wrapper.
Discard or chew the gum.

2 | Smooth the foil on a flat surface.
Flatten all wrinkles and folds.

3 | Refold the wrapper lengthwise.
Follow the existing crease lines and fold each of the longer sides up to meet in the middle, leaving the short ends unfolded.

4 | Fold the wrapper in half lengthwise.
The seams will be hidden in the middle.

5 | Fold one end into a point.

6 | Insert the point into the fold.

7 | Fit the strip around your finger in the shape of a ring.
Size the ring to a comfortable fit.

8 | Secure the ring with a small piece of tape.

Be Aware

If a gum wrapper is not available, or if you prefer a different color ring, you can use paper money. Select foreign currencies for a more dramatic palate. Other options (cut to fit) include candy bar wrappers, aluminum foil, writing paper, or bank checks.

HOW TO REVIVE
A GUEST WHO
HAS FAINTED

1 Make room around the victim.
Cool, fresh air will help to revive the guest. Do not crowd around the victim or obstruct her breathing or airway. Do not move her to another location.

2 Elevate the victim's legs.
Prop the guest's legs up on the seat of a chair or several hymn books to encourage blood flow to the head.

3 Assess the victim's breathing.
Get on your hands and knees. Observe the victim's chest: Make sure it is rising and falling rhythmically. Place your hand 2 inches above victim's nose and feel for breath. If the victim is not breathing, instruct someone nearby to call for help, then continue.

4 Check the victim's wrist for a pulse.
With your right hand, clasp the back of the victim's wrist so that your index and middle fingers lie gently over base of the palm, closer to the thumb than the pinky. Do not use your thumb to measure a pulse: The thumb can register your own pulse and mask the victim's. If you detect a pulse, skip to step 6.

5 Check for a neck pulse.
Kneel behind the victim's head so that you are looking down at her face. Using the index and middle
fingers of your right hand, gently place your fingers
under the victim's chin to the right of her Adam's
apple. Using a watch with a second hand, count
the victim's heartbeat for 15 seconds. Multiply the
number of beats by 4 to determine the number of
heartbeats per minute. If the victim's pulse is greater
than 120 or less than 50, call for help and begin CPR.
If the pulse is normal, continue to step 6.

6 Wait.
Most people faint from excessive heat, a sudden surprise, overwhelming emotion, or fatigue and will
come to on their own without treatment.

7 Mop the victim's brow with a cold, wet napkin.

8 Reposition the victim once she regains consciousness.
When she revives, help her to a chair and direct her
to keep her head between her knees. Administer non-
alcoholic drinks in small sips.

Be Aware
Smelling salts, a combination of ammonia and
strong perfume, can sometimes be effective in reviv-
ing a person who has passed out. However, they
should be used only as a last resort. Their noxious
odor may cause adverse side effects or toxicological
reactions in some people.

CHAPTER 4

RECEPTION
SURVIVAL SKILLS

HOW TO SURVIVE
THE RECEIVING LINE

⭐ Slow line
- Ask a member of the wedding party to leave the line and quietly tell a slowly moving person that someone in the other room very much wants to meet her now, then lead the slow-mover away.
- Instruct the band to relocate nearby and play very loudly so guests cannot be heard over the music and will not stop to talk.
- Insert a sweaty sous chef into the line.
- Instruct the caterers to serve food and beverages but not to get too close to the receiving line. If someone leaves the line, do not let them back in.

⭐ Chatty guest
- If a guest remains for too long, look over his shoulder, smile, and reach out your hand or cheek to greet the next guest in line, or say you will stop by the guest's table later to talk more.

⭐ Kiss on lips
- Position your face so that you are clearly offering your cheek for an air kiss.
- If a guest appears determined to make lip contact, recalculate the angle by using your ear as the target for his or her lips and turn your head sharply at the last second. Throw your arm around them to make the diversionary maneuver seem like a hug.

Dodging a Kiss

Calculate angle of approach.

Turn at last second. Throw arm to hug.

- If you know from past experience that a particular guest will lean in to kiss your lips, begin to move toward each other and then fake a cough or sneeze. When the guest momentarily pauses, rapidly move your cheek beside their cheek, completing the air kiss.
- Always keep your lips together, just in case a guest does surprise you with a direct hit.

★ Avoid a hand that's been sneezed on
- A bride should wear formal gloves in the receiving line to avoid germs from outstretched hands.
- Reach out and wrap one or both arms around the guest in a gracious hug.

★ Long bear hug
- Pat the hugger on the back. Continue increasing the force of the pats until you are released.
- Stomp on the hugger's foot. Once the hugger releases his clinch, apologize for losing your footing.
- Put your hands against the hugger's chest, stomach, or waist—whatever you can access—and push back. Do not go below the belt.
- Feign a fainting spell and transfer your total body weight onto the hugger for him to support. This will force him to recalculate his balance and give you the opportunity to step back.
- Cough in the hugger's ear.
- Give in and enjoy the moment.

★ Cheek pincher
- As the pincher approaches, drop your purse or pretend your watch fell off and quickly bend over to retrieve the object.
- Give a deep bow or curtsey, as is gender appropriate. This will result in the pincher missing his mark. Quickly turn to the next guest in line.

★ Ex-lover of spouse
- Use the "crusher" handshake. As your hand closes around your spouse's ex-lover's hand, add your other hand and exert maximum force. Smile. Grooms should not attempt if the ex is bigger and stronger.
- Pretend she is so unimportant that you do not even recognize her. Blandly say, "So nice of you to come," and briskly move on to the next person.

★ Face tired from smiling
- Turn away from your guest and do some facial exercises to loosen cramping muscles and relieve tension. Grimace fiercely, then release the expression and open your mouth and eyes wide. Slide your jaw from side to side, curl your lips around your teeth to stretch the muscles around your mouth. Use your thumbs to press under your brow bones to release tension. Turn back around and resume smiling.

HOW TO SURVIVE IF THE BAND DOESN'T SHOW UP

★ Round up street musicians.
If the reception is taking place in a city, you can also send a member of the wedding party into the subway to find musicians.

★ Call a local music school.
Send a member of the wedding party to ask for musicians who can arrive quickly. Tip them generously.

★ Play the radio.
Position a member of the wedding party at the controls of a boom box. Instruct your guests to use their mobile phones to call the radio station to make requests and dedications to the happy couple. Be prepared to change stations when necessary to avoid commercials and sad ballads.

★ Buy a CD player.
Send a member of the wedding party to purchase a CD player from a nearby electronics store. Ask guests to bring CDs from their cars.

★ Solicit musical volunteers from the crowd.
Hold a talent show, with the wedding party acting as judges.

✪ Form a jug band.

Ask guests to blow across the tops of jugs of wine or whiskey. Others can bounce sets of spoons on their leg or torso. Pots and pans from the kitchen can be beaten with spoons or other cutlery. Others can play hambone, slapping thighs, chest, and face as a rhythmical accompaniment.

Ask guests to form a jug band using available objects.

how to survive if the band doesn't show up

Replace missing band with bumping auto sound system.

⭐ Drive a small car into the reception room.
Select a car with a premier sound system, open the car doors, and blast CDs.

⭐ Borrow band members from other wedding receptions and events.
Search the facility for band members on break or who have finished performing and put together a new band for your wedding.

HOW TO STOP A
BAD TOAST

⭐ Employ humor.
Call on the same techniques hecklers use at comedy clubs: loud, insincere laughter; throwing food; and snarky commentary ("Are you going to finish this toast by their first anniversary?"). Acting drunk may also help.

⭐ Cue the band.
Ask the wedding planner or an esteemed family member to tell the band leader to interrupt with rousing music to drown out the toast.

⭐ Wait for a pause, then execute the "slow clap."
Start a loud, slow clap—approximately one clap per second. After about 15 seconds, others will join in, until the entire room is clapping for the toast maker. Continue clapping until he leaves the stage.

⭐ Talk over the toast.
Grab another microphone from the band or deejay and say, "Thanks so much for those warm wishes. Let's move on and _____ [*fill in blank with 'raise a toast,' 'cut the cake,' 'dance,' 'hear from Grandpa'*]."

★ **Ask the maid of honor to give the toast maker a big kiss.**
A passionate kiss in front of everyone will bring cheers and silence the speaker.

★ **Interrupt the toast maker with a bear hug.**
Cover the toast maker with an emotional hug while taking the microphone out of his hands and say, "Thank you so much for your kind words."

★ **Create a distraction.**
Tilt your chair and fall over backward, begin a fire at your table with candles and napkins, or drop and smash the centerpiece—any action that will derail the speaker.

Be Aware

- Schedule toasts to take place before or at the beginning of dinner. Do not wait until the cake cutting when many guests have had the opportunity to consume alcohol during cocktail hour, dinner, and dancing.
- Set a limit of three or four toasts—never have an open microphone. If other friends wish to make toasts, schedule them to take place at the rehearsal dinner.

HOW TO SURVIVE
THE FIRST DANCE
IF YOU HAVE TWO
LEFT FEET

1 Warm up.
Get comfortable moving together. Before the first dance, find a quiet space and move around the room in sync. Hold hands and move together in simple side to side and back and forth steps.

2 Dim the lights.

3 Tell the band leader to keep it short.
Inform the band of the name of your song and that you want it to end quickly. Two minutes are plenty.

4 Hold each other.
Lean lightly into your partner from the center of your body. Keep your knees soft. The groom should place his hand on the bride's shoulder blade with his fingers parallel to the floor. The bride should place her hand on the groom's right shoulder. The couple's arms should maintain contact. Make sure your legs are offset so that each foot has its own "track" to move along. The groom's chin should line up with the bride's right shoulder.

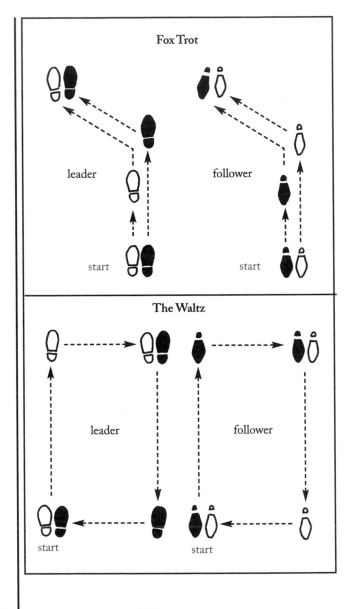

5 | Do not rush.
When the music starts, sway from side to side for a moment to feel the music. Then, on the beat, begin.

6 | Attempt a basic fox trot or waltz.
See diagrams for each step on opposite page.

7 | Whisper and laugh.
Appear to be conversing, enjoying yourselves, and joking. People will assume any missteps are the result of merriment rather than poor dancing ability.

8 | Distract the audience with a dip.
A flashy dip will focus attention on what you can do instead of what you cannot. The groom should rotate the bride sideways rather than leaning over her in the dip, both to increase the drama and for increased safety. The bride should not give the groom her entire body weight to support, and he should not dip the bride so deeply that she cannot engage her abdominal muscles to support herself.

9 | Arrange for someone to cut in.
Have the bride's father and the groom's mother cut in after 30 seconds, or fewer if you are severely challenged.

Be Aware
• Footwork is not that important, nor visible with a long wedding gown. You may improvise steps once you know the basics.

- Apply petroleum jelly to the surface of the instep of men's patent leather shoes so they will glide if they make contact.
- If you get rattled and lose the beat, recover by moving from side to side for a few moments until you both recover.
- Select a fast-tempo dance so you don't have to move together.
- Do not tango.

HOW TO REPAIR A DROPPED CAKE

Minor Shifting or Smashed Frosting

1 Smooth out rough edges with confectioners' sugar or chopped coconut.

2 Reconstruct with icing or whipped cream.
Damaged portions of a white cake may be built up and out using small amounts of buttercream or whipped cream. Apply with a spoon or butter knife. For a cake with chocolate frosting, mix slightly melted chocolate with confectioners' sugar to form a paste, then spread over the damaged area and cover as above.

3 Hide damage to the side of the cake with paper doilies.
Cut several long strips from a paper doily: The strips should match the height of the damaged layer. If necessary, use clear tape on the side that will be touching the cake to connect multiple sections. Wrap the doily around the layer and secure with small dabs of frosting. Remove the doily before serving.

4 Use fruit or nonpoisonous flowers to hide repairs.
Roses, pansies, and daisies are all nontoxic and attractive. Avoid lilies of the valley, calla lilies, and wisteria, all of which are poisonous. Place two or three large

strawberries over damaged areas, with several others around the cake to visually balance the repair.

Major Damage

1 Set aside any undamaged layers from the dropped cake.

2 Replace damaged layers.
Depending on the shape of the cake, locate rectangular or round boxes that approximately match the size of the damaged layers. Hat boxes work well for round cakes.

3 Place real cake layers on box layers.

4 Poke wooden skewers or thin dowel rods through all the layers.
Cover holes with frosting. The rods will prevent the layers from sliding, especially in warm weather.

5 Cover exposed sections of boxes with frosting as you would an actual cake.
Add flowers or other flourishes to match the existing cake.

6 Prepare to move the cake directly after cutting.
Once the first cut has been made, the cake should be taken immediately into the kitchen and the real layers sliced sparingly.

Major Cake Repairs

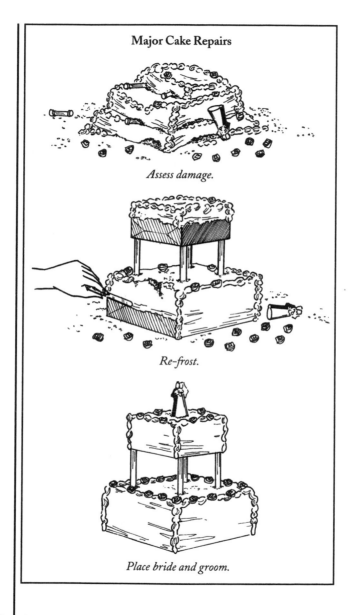

Assess damage.

Re-frost.

Place bride and groom.

Be Aware

- If the top layer of a tiered cake is damaged beyond repair, completely remove it and all support pillars, then repair remaining sections, making the next-to-the-top layer the top.
- If time permits, the caterer or pastry chef could bake or purchase a last-minute sheet cake. Serve that instead.

HOW TO AVOID A FIGHT FOR THE BOUQUET

⭐ Rig the toss.
Tell your favorite to step away from the pack. When you give her a prearranged signal, toss bouquet to her.

⭐ Split your bouquet into several individual bouquets.
Divide the bouquet into as many mini-bouquets as necessary to satisfy all the serious contenders. If there are more than four who really want the bouquet, or you're not sure how many there are, disassemble the bouquet entirely and shower the crowd.

⭐ Throw wild.
Throw the bouquet way past everyone. Throw it in the opposite direction from the crowd. Or pump fake to your left, sending the majority of women in that direction, then toss the bouquet far to your right. Once the bouquet hits the floor, the spell is broken: You need to catch the bouquet on the fly in order to be married within the year.

Be Aware
- Good spacing among the women can prevent scuffles caused by tight clustering.
- Brides should throw a secondary bouquet that is smaller and lighter and that will get better "air."

Pump left; throw right.

- The proper distance from the pack of single women is six large paces.
- You may find that no women want to catch the bouquet, for a variety of reasons. If no one steps forward, give the bouquet to the couple who has been married the longest. Alternatively, organize young girls and boys onto the dance floor and toss the bouquet to one of them.

HOW TO MAKE AN EMERGENCY GARTER

⭐ Use a scarf or bandanna.

⭐ Use a large cloth hair tie.

⭐ Use a headband.

⭐ Use a baby's head wrap.

⭐ Cut off the top of a turtleneck
Pull it on over your leg.

⭐ Use a large rubber band.
Tape tissue paper to it to make it more attractive.

⭐ Use tape.
Attach adornments to it with more tape.

⭐ Make a chain of twist ties.
Wrap around your leg and fasten the ends.

⭐ Use a silk stocking.
Cut off the foot and roll the stocking into the shape
of a garter. Make a pretty bow with excess fabric.

HOW TO BREAK UP AN ARGUMENT

⭐ Speak to the offending guests softly and slowly.
Quietly tell them that their behavior is inappropriate for a wedding, and that they must control themselves. Do not raise your voice.

⭐ Reseat the guests.
If the argumentative guests are at the same table, ask one to sit at another table.

⭐ Propose a toast.
As voices are being raised, begin tapping your glass with a spoon to signal a toast. Other guests will follow suit and the noise should drown out the shouting. The argument will be put on hold during the toast, and hopefully forgotten afterward—especially if the toast is long and boring.

⭐ Stage a dance-off.
Clear the floor of other guests and have the band play 20 seconds for each fighting guest. Use an informal survey of applause from other guests to determine the victor.

⭐ Restrain the fighting guests.
If guests are coming to blows, enlist the help of burly members of the wedding party or guests. Approach the offending guests from behind and wrap each

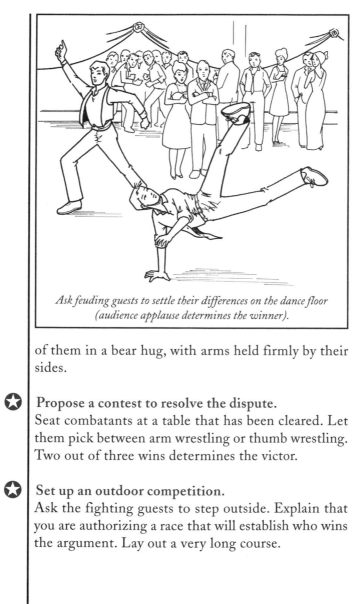

*Ask feuding guests to settle their differences on the dance floor
(audience applause determines the winner).*

of them in a bear hug, with arms held firmly by their
sides.

★ **Propose a contest to resolve the dispute.**
Seat combatants at a table that has been cleared. Let
them pick between arm wrestling or thumb wrestling.
Two out of three wins determines the victor.

★ **Set up an outdoor competition.**
Ask the fighting guests to step outside. Explain that
you are authorizing a race that will establish who wins
the argument. Lay out a very long course.

THE HONEYMOON
AND BEYOND

HOW TO DEAL WITH WEDDING NIGHT JITTERS

1 Eat.
You've probably been so busy and excited that you didn't have a chance to eat at the reception. Have some food now.

2 Postpone physical contact.
Unwind from the stress and excitement of the wedding before heading to the bedroom. Do something you both enjoy: Get an ice cream, take a stroll in a park, or just sit in a quiet place and talk about the day.

3 Eat mood-enhancing food.
Chocolate is an excellent mood enhancer: It contains the stimulants caffeine, theobromine, and phenylethylamine, as well as anandamide, a chemical—also produced naturally by the brain—that may enhance feelings of well-being.

4 Get the room ready.
Dim the lights, adjust the temperature, light scented candles, and put on soft music. Keep juices, bottled water, and fresh fruit on hand to rehydrate, rejuvenate, and reinvigorate.

5 | Get yourselves set.
The bride and groom should be relaxed, comfortable, and confident. Offer a foot rub. Use lavender soap and scent to promote relaxation. Put on a cozy nightgown or robe over sexy lingerie or underwear.

6 | Do something you've never done before.

How to Revive Your New Spouse

★ | Brew coffee.
Pass a mug of coffee repeatedly under your spouse's nose.

★ | Begin undressing your spouse.
Remove his socks to cool his body, then follow with his shirt, pants, and underwear. Most people will wake up if they sense they are being undressed.

★ | Rub ice cubes over your spouse's body.
Start with the forehead, wrists, and soles of the feet. Keep going.

★ | Apply pressure to the nail bed.
Take the tip of one of your spouse's fingers and hold it between your thumb and index finger. Very gently, apply steady pressure to the nail bed. Do not squeeze too hard. This method, used by emergency personnel to determine unconsciousness/unresponsiveness in victims, causes sharp pain. It should revive your partner quickly.

Reviving Your New Spouse

Use coffee.

Use his phone.

Use ice.

Use lung power.

★ Tickle.

★ Call on the telephone.
If you are in a hotel, call the front desk and ask them to ring your room. Or call your spouse's mobile phone from your mobile. Most people will respond to the sound of a ringing phone.

★ Pretend there is an emergency.
Yell "Fire!" "Earthquake!" "Muggers!" and "Watch out!" repeatedly to get your spouse's adrenaline flowing. Once your spouse is awake, you can explain that you weren't ready for your special night together to end.

HOW TO SURVIVE A HONEYMOON DISASTER

EXTREME SUNBURN

1 Expose damaged skin to air.
Remove all clothing around the burn area: Clothing will irritate the burn site and may cause increased pain.

2 Drink water.
Drink at least 32 ounces of water to help promote sweating, which cools the skin.

3 Apply a cold compress.
Put ice in a plastic bag, wrap in a cotton T-shirt or other fabric, and apply to the burn area. If the burn area is very large, soak a bed sheet in ice water and apply it instead of a compress. Let the skin cool under the compress for 15 minutes to help reduce pain.

4 Apply a soothing gel or ointment to the burn area.
Carefully rub a cooling aloe lotion into the burned area. This is especially soothing if the aloe has been chilled in a refrigerator or a bucket of ice. Do not apply suntan lotion, baby oil, petroleum jelly, or any other foreign substance to the burn.

5 | Take pain medication.
Ibuprofen will help reduce pain at the burn site.

6 | Lie still.
Lie in a position that best exposes your sunburn to the air without coming into contact with the bed, your clothing, or another person. Do not bend sunburned joints.

7 | Continue with your honeymoon.
Take advantage of loose-fitting island fashions as your sunburn heals.

Be Aware
Depending on the severity of the sunburn, a new layer of skin will replace the burned area in two days to two weeks.

MIGRAINE HEADACHE

1 | Dim the lights.
Bright lights may exacerbate a migraine or prolong symptoms. Keep the shades drawn and the room lights off or very low.

2 | Reduce noise levels.
Turn off the radio and television. The room should be silent, or with soothing "white" noise such as that created by a small fan.

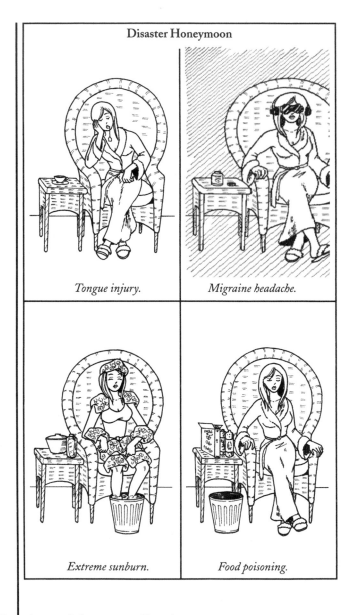

Disaster Honeymoon

Tongue injury.

Migraine headache.

Extreme sunburn.

Food poisoning.

3 | Limit movement.
Running, walking, and even climbing stairs may increase the intensity of a migraine.

4 | Eat vitamin-rich foods.
Magnesium and vitamin B2 (riboflavin) may combat migraine symptoms. Spinach, Swiss chard, and many nuts are high in magnesium, while mackerel, shad, and other oily fish are rich in riboflavin.

Be Aware
A migraine may last as little as one hour or as long as three days.

ACUTE TONGUE INJURY

1 | Prepare a tea bag.
Soak a tea bag in warm water for 2 minutes. Let it stand 1 minute at room temperature, then wrap it in gauze or a clean cloth napkin.

2 | Apply tea bag to tongue.
Place the moist tea bag on the injury site and press steadily. The tannic acid in the tea is a natural coagulant and should stop the bleeding. The tongue has a large number of blood vessels near the surface and will bleed profusely until the blood coagulates.

3 | Rinse.
Swish and spit using an anesthetic mouthwash, if available.

4 | Apply a numbing agent.
Apply ice to the wound to numb and reduce pain.

5 | Avoid acidic and salty foods and liquids.
Acidic substances, such as citrus fruits and vinegar, and those high in salt, such as nuts and potato chips, may aggravate the injury.

6 | Keep the tongue still.
The tongue will heal more quickly if it is inactive.

7 | Protect the tongue.
Wear an athletic mouth guard to protect the tongue until the injury heals.

FOOD POISONING

1 | Stay hydrated.
Drink several gallons of water a day.

2 | Replenish mineral salts.
Nibble on dry salted crackers or plain rice to replace salt lost through diarrhea.

3 | Do not induce vomiting.
Vomiting will not remove the bacterial culprit, but will cause dehydration.

Be Aware

- Do not drink the water when traveling to the tropics or when you are unsure of its cleanliness. Avoid ice cubes in drinks, brushing your teeth with tap water, opening your mouth in the shower, or swallowing—or even rinsing your mouth with—water in swimming pools or the ocean.

- Only eat fruit that you can peel yourself. Avoid all vegetables and fruits that could have been washed in contaminated water, or fruits (like melons) that might have been soaked in water to increase their size and weight.

- If you don't know what it is, don't eat it.

HOW TO REPURPOSE UNWANTED GIFTS

If an undesirable gift is monogrammed, handmade with nowhere to be returned, of an unknown origin, used before a better version arrived, from a relative who will ask about the gift when visiting your home, from a store that will no longer accept it as a return, or from a store that is no longer in business, you will need to find a way to put it to use in your home.

⭐ Candlesticks
- Place under your bed to keep sagging mattress firm.
- Use as lipstick holders on a crowded vanity.
- Use as paper clip holders on a desk.
- Use as tall saltcellars on the dining room table.

⭐ Bowl
- Use as a litter box. Make sure it is stable.
- Use as a sock bin.
- Use as a potty chair.

⭐ Blender
- Use as a flower vase.
- Use as a paper shredder.

⭐ Flower vase
- Use as a pen/pencil holder near a phone.
- Use as a beer mug or water glass.

★ Crockpot
- Use as a wax warmer for depilatory waxing.
- Use as an ice bucket (unplugged).
- Use as a planter for tropical plants (plugged in).

★ Gardener's wheelbarrow
- Use as a shopping cart.
- Use as a laundry basket.
- Use as a stroller for a baby.

★ Ironing board
- Use as a toboggan.
- Use as a table.

Be Aware

Even if you do not like the gift, you must still send a thank-you note. Thank the giver for the gesture and thoughtfulness. See the Gift Evaluator/Thank-You Note Generator on page 162.

HOW TO SURVIVE IF YOU FORGET YOUR ANNIVERSARY

★ Order an emergency bouquet.
Many florists can assemble arrangements with little notice. If you have just minutes to prepare, scour your neighborhood flowerbeds for daisies. Wrap them in colorful ribbon and present them as your initial gift.

★ Buy chocolates.
Most supermarkets and drugstores carry chocolate assortments. Choose a tasteful boxed set rather than several loose candy bars tied with ribbon.

★ Create a voucher card.
Prepare a card or piece of paper that shows the wonderful gift you're giving but can't give now because it isn't ready yet. Draw a picture of the gift on the card or paper.

★ Apologize, apologize, apologize.
If you're caught with nothing, making excuses will not help your case. Your level of contrition should be so extreme that your spouse begins to feel bad because you feel so terrible.

⭐ Give an intangible present.
Give her a homemade certificate for a weekend spa getaway. It could be for her only, or for a romantic weekend for both of you—a "second honeymoon" (but don't push your luck). A week free of household chores, a weekend of breakfasts in bed, or getting her car detailed are other possibilities.

HOW TO SLEEP ON THE COUCH

1 Remove the back cushions.
If the couch has loose back cushions, take them off to add more width to the sleeping surface.

2 Remove the arm cushions.
Side cushions take up precious head and leg room, and will just end up on the floor in the middle of the night anyway.

3 Fluff and flip.
If the sofa design permits, remove the seat cushions, fluff them, then flip them so the side that was down is now the top. This will provide a more even sleeping surface.

4 Cover the seat cushions with a sheet.
The sheet will protect your face from odors trapped in the cushions and will protect the seating area from saliva.

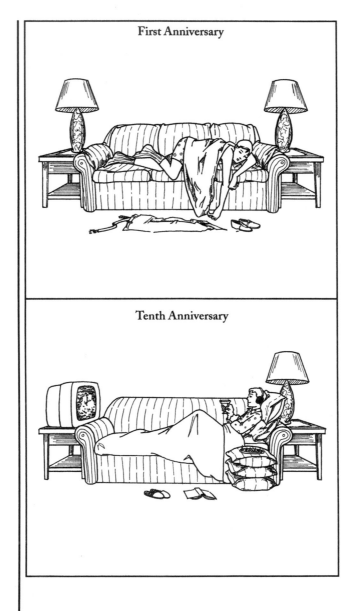

First Anniversary

Tenth Anniversary

chapter 5: the honeymoon and beyond

5 | Use your usual pillow.
You will sleep better with your head resting on a familiar pillow. Get yours from the bedroom, if the bedroom is still accessible to you.

6 | Depending on the temperature of the room and your comfort level, get a sheet, blanket, comforter, or large towel to put on top of you.

7 | Relax.
Do not to go to bed angry.

Be Aware

If you are an active sleeper, lay the sofa cushions next to the sofa to break your fall should you roll off during the night.

APPENDIX

WEDDING SURVIVAL CHECKLISTS

Make sure you have these items.

Walking-Down-the-Aisle Survival Checklist
- ❑ Bride
- ❑ Veil
- ❑ Wedding dress
- ❑ Shoes (hers)
- ❑ Maid of honor
- ❑ Bridesmaids
- ❑ Someone to give the bride away
- ❑ Groom
- ❑ Tuxedo/suit
- ❑ Shoes (his)
- ❑ Best man
- ❑ Rings
- ❑ Petroleum jelly (in case ring won't fit)
- ❑ Chewing gum (use wrappers to make emergency rings)
- ❑ Groomsmen
- ❑ Officiant
- ❑ Emergency vows (in case officiant forgets)
- ❑ Small paper bag (to alleviate hyperventilation)
- ❑ Flask with alcohol (for courage)
- ❑ Tranquilizers
- ❑ Smelling salts

Reception Survival Checklist
- ❑ Food
- ❑ Liquor
- ❑ Place to put presents
- ❑ Formal gloves (to block reception line germs)
- ❑ Butter (to soothe chapped lips from kissing)
- ❑ Photographer

- ❏ Garter
- ❏ Scarf (to use as emergency garter)
- ❏ Tables
- ❏ Chairs
- ❏ Napkins
- ❏ Cake
- ❏ Band
- ❏ Small car with loud sound system (to replace missing band)
- ❏ Petroleum jelly (apply to insteps for gliding dance moves)
- ❏ Duct tape and shot glasses (to replace shoe heel)
- ❏ Electrical tape (to make tuxedo stripe on pants)
- ❏ Insect repellant (for outdoor weddings)
- ❏ Tranquilizers
- ❏ Smelling salts

Honeymoon Survival Checklist
- ❏ Airline tickets
- ❏ Toothbrushes
- ❏ Toothpaste
- ❏ Straw hats (for hot climates)
- ❏ Hats with earflaps (for cold climates)
- ❏ Insect repellant (for tropical climates)
- ❏ Flashlight
- ❏ Sunscreen
- ❏ Aloe (to treat sunburn)
- ❏ Aspirin (for headaches)
- ❏ Ice pack (for headaches, sunburns, and sprains)
- ❏ Tea bags (to soothe swollen eyes and tongue)
- ❏ Petroleum jelly
- ❏ Bottled water (for sunburn, upset stomach)
- ❏ Antacids (for upset stomach)
- ❏ Club soda (for upset stomach)
- ❏ Crackers (for upset stomach)
- ❏ Sexy lingerie
- ❏ Smelling salts
- ❏ Tranquilizers

GIFT EVALUATOR/ THANK-YOU NOTE GENERATOR

Use the following equation and score chart to assess the ACTUAL VALUE (AV) of any wedding gift; then select the appropriate thank-you note.

$$\text{V/GI} \times (\text{T}_Q + \text{A}_Q) = \text{AV}$$

 V = Estimated retail value
   (in dollars)
 GI = Estimated gross annual income of giver
   (in thousands of dollars)
 T$_Q$ = Tastefulness quotient (from tacky to attractive
   to classy, on a scale of 1–10)

Tacky	Attractive	Classy
1	5	10

A$_Q$ = Appropriateness quotient (from dumb to useful
   to cool, on a scale of 1– 10)

Dumb	Useful	Cool
1	5	10

AV = ACTUAL VALUE

Example:

You are given a blender with a retail value around $100 by a college friend with a gross annual income of around $40,000. It is quite tasteful in design (you'd rate it a 9 in T$_Q$ as blenders go) and will be quite useful (a 9 as well, since you don't have a blender).

Thus, this gift receives a score of:
100/40 x (9 + 9) = 45, a high score.

If you received the same gift from a wealthy family friend, however, with a gross annual income around $140,000, the gift would receive a score of:

100/140 x (9 + 9) = 12.86, a low score.

You are given a doormat with a retail value around $35 by a neighbor with a gross annual income of around $100,000. It's hideously ugly (a TQ rating of 2), and you already have a doormat (AQ rating of 3, as there would be some pleasure in wiping your feet on it).

35/100 x (2 + 3) = 1.75, a score below the scale.

Score Chart
Below 10 . . . . . A very bad gift—no note
10–20 . . . . A bad gift—use Note A
21–40 . . . . A good gift—use Note B
41+ . . . . A great gift—use Note C

Note A

Dear _____,

Thank you so much for the *[name of gift here]*. We can't believe you thought of it for us! We will put it in a special place. Know that whenever we look at it, we'll think of you.

Sincerely,

[your names here]

Note B

Dear _____,

Thank you so much for the *[name of gift here]*. We genuinely appreciate your thoughtfulness in seeking out such a practical and appropriate gift. Just know that whenever we use it, we'll think of you.

Sincerely,

[your names here]

Note C

Dear _____,

Thank you so much for the *[name of gift here]*. We can't believe your generosity and creativity. It's a fabulous gift. You must come over and enjoy it with us soon. We think of you always.

Sincerely,

[your names here]

THE EXPERTS

Sherry Amatenstein is the dating columnist at iVillage and the author of *Love Lessons from Bad Breakups* (www.luvlessons.com). She lives in New York.

Kristi Amoroso owns Kristi Amoroso Special Events (www.kristiamoroso.com), a wedding planning, event design, and production management company serving Napa, Sonoma, San Francisco, and the Bay Area.

Liz Applegate, Ph.D., is a faculty member of the Nutrition Department at the University of California, Davis, and the author of several books, including *Eat Smart, Play Hard* and *Bounce Your Body Beautiful: 6 Weeks to a Sexier, Firmer Body.*

Sharon Ashe, along with her partner, Paul Overton, has been helping couples prepare for their first dance for almost a decade. Their North Carolina–based company, Now You're Dancing (www.nowyouredancing.com), was founded on the idea that dancing at your wedding can be fun and easy for everyone involved.

Karen Boehne is a second-generation dry cleaner with more than 37 years of experience in the field. She is a graduate of the International Fabricare Industry general dry-cleaning course and is currently the president of Minnesota Cleaners Association. Boehne cleans, restores, presses, and preserves wedding gowns at Wedding Gown Care Specialists (www.WeddingGownCareSpecialist.com) in New Hope, Minnesota.

Gloria Brame, Ph.D., M.P.H.H.S. (www.gloria-brame.com), is a clinical sexologist in private practice and a member of the American College of Sexologists. She lives and works in Athens, Georgia.

Jennifer Brisman is president of jennifer brisman weddings newyork, inc (www.theweddingplanner.com).

Byron Burge owns Advanced Air Solutions (www.advancedairsolutions.com), a company specializing in air filtration and purification systems, which supplies smoke and odor removal equipment to private homes, restaurants, cigar stores, smoking clubs, and other commercial establishments throughout the world.

Sharlene A. Caldwell is co-owner of White Glove Event Production, LLC (www.whitegloveep.com), based in Roanoke, Virginia. She and her business partner, Caroline Hammond, have varied experience, including work in the fields of advertising, fashion, and catering, which has equipped them with unique insight that has made their company one of the area's top firms.

Phyllis Cambria has been a wedding and event planner for more than 20 years. Her advice has appeared in *The Knot*, *Weddingpages*, and numerous other bridal publications. Together with her partner, Patty Sachs, she co-wrote *The Pocket Idiot's Guide to Choosing a Caterer* and *The Complete Idiot's Guide to Throwing a Great Party* and co-owns WeddingPlansPlus.com.

Sally Lorensen Conant, Ph.D., operates Orange Restoration Labs, the largest gown preservation service in New England. She is the administrative vice president of the Association of Wedding Gown Specialists (www.WeddingGownSpecialist.com/emergencygowncare.htm), a not-for-profit trade association of cleaners in the United States, Canada, and Australia who specialize in cleaning heirloom textiles of all types. Often featured in wedding books and magazines, Conant is recognized by the Association of Bridal Consultants as a "Master Wedding Vendor."

Tracey Ellenbogen, M.S.W., L.C.S.W., runs Calling All Brides, a stress management workshop for brides who are overwhelmed with the stress of wedding planning and preparing for marriage. She is a licensed psychotherapist in private practice in Bala Cynwyd, Pennsylvania.

Robbi Ernst III is a wedding planner, wedding consultant, and the founder of June Wedding Inc. (www.junewedding.com), an association for event-planning professionals. He is the author of *Great Wedding Tips from the Experts.*

Leslie Hafter, a mother of two, has been making gum wrapper rings, necklaces, and bracelets for 25 years. She lives in suburban Philadelphia.

Richard Hafter, D.D.S., is a dentist in private practice in Hammonton, New Jersey.

Caroline Hammond is co-owner of White Glove Event Production, LLC (www.whitegloveep.com), based in Roanoke, Virginia. She and her business partner, Sharlene A. Caldwell, have varied experience, including work in the fields of advertising, fashion, and catering, which has equipped them with unique insight that has made their company one of the area's top firms.

Seth Haplea, M.D., is a neurologist in private practice in Chadds Ford, Pennsylvania.

Tobias Haslam-Hopwood, Psy.D., is a licensed clinical psychologist and an assistant professor in the Menninger Department of Psychiatry at the Baylor College of Medicine in Houston, Texas.

Melisa W. Lai., M.D., is emergency medicine attending physician at Mt. Auburn Hospital in Cambridge, Massachusetts, and a fellow in clinical toxicology at the Massachusetts/Rhode Island Poison Control Center.

Sherry Maysonave is president of Empowerment Enterprises (www.casualpower.com), a firm specializing in image and communication, and the author of *Casual Power: How to Power Up Your Nonverbal Communication and Dress Down for Success.*

National Center for Health Statistics, part of the U.S. Centers for Disease Control and Prevention.

Tom Ogren (www.allergyfreegardening.com), a horticulturist who consults for the U.S. Department of Agriculture on the connections between landscape plants and allergies, is the author of several books, including *Safe Sex in the Garden*. He lives in California.

Paul Overton, along with his partner, Sharon Ashe, has been helping couples prepare for their first dance for almost a decade. Their North Carolina–based company, Now You're Dancing (www.nowyouredancing.com), was founded on the idea that dancing at your wedding can be fun and easy for everyone involved.

Melissa Paul is founder and creative director of Melissa Paul LTD (www.melissapaul.com). She is the Philadelphia local expert for theknot.com and contributing editor to *Weddingpages* magazine and *The Knot Book of Wedding Flowers*. An active member in the Association of Bridal Consultants and the National Association of Catering Executives, she is also co-chair for the Association of Bridal Consultants Greater Philadelphia Branch.

Sarah Phillips, a former gourmet food broker, created the Healthy Oven line of baking mixes. She is the author of *Baking 9-1-1* and runs Baking911.com.

Peggy Post is the author of 10 books on etiquette, including *Emily Post's Etiquette* and *Emily Post's Wedding Etiquette*. Millions seek her advice through monthly columns in *Good Housekeeping* and *Parents* magazines, her wedding postings on WeddingChannel.com, columns in *InStyle Weddings*, and by visiting the Emily Post Institute Website (www.emily-post.com).

BethAnn Schacht, L.M.H.C. (www.thebridalcoach.com), is a life coach and licensed therapist in the Boston area. The unexpected stress of her own engagement led her to explore the emotional journey of getting married, and she now works with brides and couples to refocus the wedding planning around their relationship and personal values.

Brian Shapiro is the third-generation president of the Cigar Factory Outlet (www.discountcigars.com) in South Norwalk, Connecticut, which sells and distributes fine cigars world-wide. His family has been in the cigar business since 1932.

Jodi R. R. Smith has been working with organizations, corporations, educational institutions, and individuals since 1986 to increase their social savvy and confidence levels. In 1996, she founded Mannersmith (www.mannersmith.com), an etiquette-consulting firm that creates and delivers seminars to clients ranging from children to CEOs.

Sasha Souza established her company, Sasha Souza Events (www.sashasouza.com), in 1995, specializing in full-service wedding and event design and coordination. Sasha Souza Events has offices in the Beverly Hills and Napa Valley areas and is a distinguished member and accredited bridal consultant with the Association of Bridal Consultants (ABC) and a member of International Special Events Society (ISES).

Liz Stewart owns Liz Stewart Inspired Floral Design (www.lizflowers.com) in Jacksonville, Florida, and has been designing arrangements for weddings and other events for 16 years. She is also a member of the American Friends of Versailles, a select group of U.S. florists that does floral design at the Chateau de Versailles in France.

Elaine Tse launched her company, Tselaine Jewelry (www.tselaine.com), several years ago and creates distinct lines of handmade jewelry.

Mara J. Urshel is owner/president of Kleinfeld Bridal (www.kleinfeldbridal.com), located in Brooklyn, New York. With 30 years of experience in luxury merchandise, Urshel directs all merchandising, sales, marketing, and advertising at Kleinfeld Bridal. She is the co-author of *How to Buy Your Perfect Wedding Dress*.

ABOUT THE AUTHORS

Joshua Piven's wedding featured a flower girl temper tantrum, bad catering, and the happy couple's impressive performance of "The Hustle." He is the co-author, with David Borgenicht, of the *Worst-Case Scenario Survival Handbook* series. Still happily married, he and his family live in Philadelphia.

David Borgenicht is a writer and book publisher whose own wedding took place more than nine years ago. At the wedding, he survived nightmare rabbis, marathon toasting, excessive drunkenness, and a cousin who ate the chocolate flowers off the cake before it was served. It was a wonderful occasion.

Sarah Jordan is a National Magazine Award–nominated writer whose wedding featured a band so committed to entertaining that they refused to stop playing so guests could leave the dance floor for dessert. Co-author of *The Worst-Case Scenario Survival Handbook: Parenting*, she lives in Philadelphia with her family.

Brenda Brown is an illustrator and cartoonist whose work has been published in many books and major publications, including *The Worst-Case Scenario Survival Handbook* series, *Esquire*, *Reader's Digest*, *USA Weekend*, *21st Century Science & Technology*, *The Saturday Evening Post*, *The National Enquirer*, and many other magazines. Her Website is http://webtoon.com.

Visit www.worstcasescenarios.com for updates, new scenarios, and more! Because you just never know . . .

ACKNOWLEDGMENTS

Joshua Piven thanks everyone involved for the wonderful memories: co-authors, editors, experts, caterers, florists, pastry chefs, bartenders, and, of course, the band. Expect a thank-you note in six to nine months.

David Borgenicht would like to thank everyone who contributed to making this magical night—er, book—happen: his co-authors, Josh and Sarah; his editors, Jay Schaefer, Steve Mockus, and Melissa "Wedding Planner" Wagner; perennial *Worst-Case* designer Frances J. Soo Ping Chow; and all of the experts whose knowledge makes the world a safer, saner place.

Sarah Jordan thanks all the experts who shared their wisdom and insights into how to prevent a wedding disaster; she also thanks her family, Jessica Capizzi, and Cadence Berns.

MORE WORST-CASE SCENARIOS

The Worst-Case Scenario Survival Handbook

The Worst-Case Scenario Survival Handbook: Travel

*The Worst-Case Scenario
Survival Handbook: Dating & Sex*

The Worst-Case Scenario Survival Handbook: Golf

The Worst-Case Scenario Survival Handbook: Holidays

The Worst-Case Scenario Survival Handbook: Work

*The Worst-Case Scenario
Survival Handbook: Parenting*

The Worst-Case Scenario Survival Handbook: College

———————

The Worst-Case Scenario Survival Calendar

The Worst-Case Scenario Daily Survival Calendar

The Worst-Case Scenario Survival Journal

The Worst-Case Scenario Survival Cards: 30 Postcards

The Worst-Case Scenario Dating & Sex Address Book

The Worst-Case Scenario Holiday Survival Cards

The Worst-Case Scenario Work Sticky Situation Notes